Domestic Abuse and the European Court of Human Rights

This book provides a detailed critical analysis of the jurisprudence of the European Court of Human Rights on domestic abuse. Such abuse affects vast numbers of people throughout all nations of the world. Although it was not until 2007 that domestic abuse was considered substantively by the European Court of Human Rights, it has now been established that such abuse can constitute a violation of the right to life under Article 2 of the European Convention on Human Rights; the right to be free from torture or inhuman or degrading treatment under Article 3; the right to respect for private and family life under Article 8; and the prohibition of discrimination under Article 14. The book analyses how conceptualisations of domestic abuse in the Court's jurisprudence have evolved, for example, in relation to a more consistent use of Article 3 in such cases, a recognition of coercive control, and the framing of domestic abuse as gender-based discrimination. It also explores the development of the Court's understanding of domestic abuse, for example, as regards to how the '*Osman* test' should be applied in this context. Additionally, the book discusses the Court's approach to issues such as cyber violence and child contact in the context of domestic abuse. The book will appeal to academics and researchers from a wide variety of disciplines, such as criminal law, criminology, social policy, human rights, family law, gender studies and sociology, as well as practitioners and those in the voluntary sector who are working in the area of combating domestic abuse. The book could also be used beneficially on courses at both undergraduate and postgraduate levels which incorporate the topic of domestic abuse.

Ronagh J.A. McQuigg is a Reader in the School of Law, Queen's University Belfast. Her research interests are in the area of International Human Rights Law, and she currently teaches in the areas of Land Law and Family Law.

Routledge Research in Human Rights Law

The Right of the Child to Play
From Conception to Implementation
Naomi Lott

Social Media, Fundamental Rights and Courts
A European Perspective
Edited by Federica Casarosa and Evangelia Psychogiopoulou

Housing, Land and Property Rights
Residential Justice, Conflict Zones and Climate Change
Scott Leckie

The European Convention on Human Rights and the COVID-19 Pandemic
Ronagh J.A. McQuigg

International Human Rights and Local Courts
Human Rights Interpretation in Indonesia
Edited by Aksel Tømte and Eko Riyadi

Defamation and the Right to Freedom of Speech
The UK in Comparative Perspective
Mariette Jones

Bulk Surveillance, Democracy and Human Rights Law in Europe
A Comparative Perspective
Marcin Rojszczak

Surveillance Law, Data Retention and Human Rights
A Risk to Democracy
Matthew White

Domestic Abuse and the European Court of Human Rights
Ronagh J.A. McQuigg

For more information about this series, please visit: www.routledge.com/Routledge-Research-in-Human-Rights-Law/book-series/HUMRIGHTSLAW

Domestic Abuse and the European Court of Human Rights

Ronagh J.A. McQuigg

Routledge
Taylor & Francis Group
LONDON AND NEW YORK

First published 2025
by Routledge
4 Park Square, Milton Park, Abingdon, Oxon OX14 4RN

and by Routledge
605 Third Avenue, New York, NY 10158

Routledge is an imprint of the Taylor & Francis Group, an informa business

British Library Cataloguing-in-Publication Data
A catalogue record for this book is available from the British Library

Library of Congress Cataloging-in-Publication Data
Names: McQuigg, Ronagh J. A., author.
Title: Domestic abuse and the European Court of Human Rights / Ronagh J.A. McQuigg.
Description: Abingdon, Oxon [UK]; New York, NY: Routledge, 2025. | Series: Routledge research in human rights law | Includes bibliographical references and index. | Identifiers: LCCN 2024036921 (print) | LCCN 2024036922 (ebook) | ISBN 9781032778396 (hardback) | ISBN 9781032796246 (hardback) | ISBN 9781003493068 (ebook)
Subjects: LCSH: Family violence–Law and legislation–Europe. | International law and human rights–Europe. | Human rights–Europe. | European Court of Human Rights. | Convention for the Protection of Human Rights and Fundamental Freedoms (1950 November 5) | Council of Europe Convention on Preventing and Combating Violence against Women and Domestic Violence (2011 May 11)
Classification: LCC KJC8385.F36 M35 2025 (print) | LCC KJC8385.F36 (ebook) | DDC 342.2408/5–dc23/eng/20240813
LC record available at https://lccn.loc.gov/2024036921
LC ebook record available at https://lccn.loc.gov/2024036922

ISBN: 978-1-032-77839-6 (hbk)
ISBN: 978-1-032-79624-6 (pbk)
ISBN: 978-1-003-49306-8 (ebk)

DOI: 10.4324/9781003493068

Typeset in Times New Roman
by Deanta Global Publishing Services, Chennai, India

Contents

1 Introduction and Context

This book seeks to provide an in-depth critical analysis of the jurisprudence of the European Court of Human Rights (ECtHR) on the issue of domestic abuse. Such abuse affects vast numbers of people in all nations and is an issue which has recently been brought even more clearly into focus, given that levels of domestic abuse increased substantially around the world since the onset of the COVID-19 pandemic.[1] Traditionally, domestic abuse was not an issue viewed as falling within the ambit of international human rights law, which was originally formulated to protect the rights of the individual from encroachment by the state. Nevertheless, through the development of the concepts of state responsibility and positive obligations, human rights law has now evolved so that in certain circumstances states have obligations to protect the rights of individuals from being violated through the actions of third parties, such as in situations involving domestic abuse. For example, in its General Recommendations Nos. 19[2] and 35,[3] the UN Committee on the Elimination of Discrimination Against Women (CEDAW Committee) has interpreted the UN Convention on the Elimination of All Forms of Discrimination Against Women (CEDAW), which contains no express reference to violence against women in such a manner as to encompass such violence in both the public and private spheres. Such developments are not, of course, confined to the UN but can also be seen within regional systems such as the Council of Europe, in which, for example, the Convention on Preventing and Combating Violence Against Women and Domestic Violence (Istanbul Convention) was adopted in 2011.

However, the focus of this book is on developments in the case law of the ECtHR on domestic abuse. Remarkably, it was not until 2007 that such

1 UN Women, 'Measuring the Shadow Pandemic: Violence against Women during COVID-19', 4 November 2021, https://data.unwomen.org/publications/vaw-rga.

2 UN Committee on the Elimination of Discrimination Against Women, 'General Recommendation No. 19: Violence against women' (1992).

3 UN Committee on the Elimination of Discrimination Against Women, 'General Recommendation No. 35: Gender-based violence against women' (2017).

DOI: 10.4324/9781003493068-1

abuse was considered substantively by the Court.[4] Nevertheless, through the application of the concept of positive obligations, it has now been established that domestic abuse can constitute a violation of the right to life under Article 2 of the European Convention on Human Rights (ECHR),[5] the right to be free from torture or inhuman or degrading treatment under Article 3,[6] the right to respect for private and family life under Article 8[7] and the prohibition of discrimination found in Article 14.[8] Developments such as the adoption of the Istanbul Convention and the multitude of documents issued by various UN bodies regarding domestic abuse as a human rights issue are, of course, immensely significant. However, the ECHR is one of the few international or regional human rights instruments with a judicial enforcement mechanism, and indeed, the ECtHR has been described as 'the crown jewel of the world's most advanced international system for protecting civil and political liberties'.[9] As Fraser remarks, the ECtHR is 'a unique body that has played a pivotal role in strengthening the protection of human rights across Europe'.[10] Likewise Bradley comments that 'this body has been the foremost regional mechanism in the world for enabling disputed questions of fundamental rights to be decided in a judicial forum'.[11] The approach of the ECtHR to the issue of domestic abuse is therefore of great importance and merits detailed exploration and analysis.

This chapter begins by discussing how domestic abuse is defined and then proceeds to place the ECtHR's jurisprudence on domestic abuse in context by providing a brief overview of how international human rights law has evolved to encompass this issue, and an outline of developments in this respect within the UN and regional human rights systems. The chapter then introduces the ECHR itself and the concept of positive obligations which has been crucial

4 *Kontrova v. Slovakia* (App. No. 7510/04), judgment of 31 May 2007.

5 For example, *Y and Others v. Bulgaria* (App. No. 9077/18), judgment of 22 March 2022.

6 For example, *Tunikova and Others v. Russia* (App. Nos. 55974/16, 53118/17, 27484/18, 28011/19), judgment of 14 December 2021.

7 For example, *Bevacqua and S v. Bulgaria* (App. No. 71127/01), judgment of 12 June 2008.

8 For example, *Tkhelidze v. Georgia* (App. No. 33056/17), judgment of 8 July 2021.

9 Helfer L.R., 'Redesigning the European Court of Human Rights: Embeddedness as a Deep Structural Principle of the European Human Rights Regime' (2008) 19 *European Journal of International Law* 125 at 125.

10 Fraser J., 'Conclusion: The European Convention on Human Rights as a common European endeavour' in Flogaitis S., Zwart T. and Fraser J. (eds), *The European Court of Human Rights and its Discontents – Turning Criticism into Strength*, 2013, Edward Elgar Publishing, Cheltenham, 192 at 192.

11 Bradley A., 'Introduction: The need for both international and national protection of human rights – the European challenge' in Flogaitis S., Zwart T. and Fraser J. (eds), *The European Court of Human Rights and its Discontents – Turning Criticism into Strength*, 2013, Edward Elgar Publishing, Cheltenham, 1 at 2.

in addressing the issue of domestic abuse. In addition, an outline of the forthcoming chapters is provided.

What Is Domestic Abuse?

Article 3(b) of the Istanbul Convention defines 'domestic violence' as encompassing 'all acts of physical, sexual, psychological or economic violence that occur within the family or domestic unit or between former or current spouses or partners, whether or not the perpetrator shares or has shared the same residence with the victim'.[12] Women's Aid defines domestic abuse in a similar manner as 'an incident or pattern of incidents of controlling, coercive, threatening, degrading and violent behaviour, including sexual violence, in the majority of cases by a partner or ex-partner, but also by a family member or carer'.[13]

Nevertheless, it is important to note that conceptualisations of domestic abuse have evolved over time. For many years, such abuse was viewed as being synonymous with physical violence. For example, in the UK, until relatively recently, incidents of domestic abuse had to be prosecuted under general criminal law statutes such as the Offences Against the Person Act 1861. This was relatively unproblematic regarding incidents of physical violence, as these could be prosecuted under the 1861 Act as, for instance, common assault under section 42, aggravated assault under section 43, assault occasioning actual bodily harm under section 47, assault occasioning grievous bodily harm under section 18 or unlawful wounding under section 20. In *R v. Ireland and R v. Burstow*[14] it was held that a recognisable psychiatric illness could constitute 'bodily harm' for the purposes of sections 18, 20 and 47 of the Offences Against the Person Act. Nevertheless, states of mind which are not supported by medical evidence of psychiatric injury are not encompassed by the 1861 legislation.

However, it has now been recognised that domestic abuse encompasses not only physical violence but also 'coercive control' more broadly.[15] As Herring remarks, 'The concept of coercive control is an attempt to identify one of the

12 The Istanbul Convention uses the term 'domestic violence', as opposed to 'domestic abuse'.

13 Women's Aid, 'What is domestic abuse?', https://www.womensaid.org.uk/information-support/what-is-domestic-abuse/.

14 [1997] 4 All ER 225.

15 For a discussion of the concept of coercive control, see Stark E., *Coercive Control: How Men Trap Women in Personal Life*, 2007, Oxford University Press, Oxford; Stark E., 'Rethinking Coercive Control' (2009) 15 *Violence Against Women* 1509; Williamson E., 'Living in the World of the Domestic Violence Perpetrator: Negotiating the Unreality of Coercive Control' (2010) 16 *Violence Against Women* 1412; Stark E., 'Looking Beyond Domestic Violence: Policing Coercive Control' (2012) 12 *Journal of Police Crisis Negotiations* 199; and Stark E. and Hester M., 'Coercive Control: Update and Review' (2019) 25 *Violence Against Women* 81.

wrongs at the heart of domestic abuse. It does so by showing that domestic abuse is a particular kind of relationship rather than being a particular kind of act'.[16] Fitz-Gibbon, Walklate and McCulloch comment that, 'Coercive control illuminates domestic abuse as a pattern of behaviours, within which physical violence may exist alongside a range of other abusive behaviours'.[17] As Women's Aid states, 'Coercive control creates invisible chains and a sense of fear that pervades all elements of a victim's life. It works to limit their human rights by depriving them of their liberty and reducing their ability for action'.[18] The tactics of perpetrators of coercive control may include emotional abuse such as blaming the victim or undermining her self-esteem and self-worth; verbal abuse such as humiliation and degradation; systematic social isolation; economic abuse, for example, controlling all finances; threats and intimidation; and physical abuse.[19] As Herring comments, 'Fear is often at the heart of coercive control and is its primary vehicle. Violence may or may not be used as one tool'.[20] Due to such considerations, coercive and controlling behaviour was criminalised in England and Wales under section 76 of the Serious Crime Act 2015;[21] abusive behaviour (including psychological abuse) towards a partner or ex-partner was criminalised in Scotland under section 1 of the Domestic Abuse (Scotland) Act 2018;[22] and a domestic abuse offence that essentially criminalised coercive and controlling behaviour was

16 Herring J., *Domestic Abuse and Human Rights*, 2020, Intersentia, Cambridge, at 26.

17 Fitz-Gibbon K., Walklate S. and McCulloch J., 'Editorial Introduction', (2018) 18 *Criminology and Criminal Justice* 3 at 3.

18 Women's Aid, 'What is Coercive Control?', https://www.womensaid.org.uk/information-support/what-is-domestic-abuse/coercive-control/.

19 Jeffries S., 'In the Best Interests of the Abuser: Coercive Control, Child Custody Proceedings and the "Expert" Assessments that Guide Judicial Determinations' (2016) 5 *Laws* 14 at 15.

20 Herring, op. cit., at 27.

21 For a discussion of section 76 of the Serious Crime Act 2015, see Bettinson V. and Robson J., 'Prosecuting Coercive Control: Reforming Storytelling in the Courtroom' (2020) 12 *Criminal Law Review* 1107; McGorrery P. and McMahon M., 'Criminalising "the worst" part: operationalising the offence of coercive control in England and Wales' (2019) 11 *Criminal Law Review* 957; Bettinson V., 'Aligning partial defences to murder with the offence of coercive or controlling behaviour' (2019) 83 *Journal of Criminal Law* 71; and Bishop C. and Bettinson V., 'Evidencing domestic violence, including behaviour that falls under the new offence of "coercive and controlling behaviour"' (2018) 22 *International Journal of Evidence and Proof* 3.

22 For a discussion of the Domestic Abuse (Scotland) Act 2018, see Cairns I., 'The *Moorov* doctrine and coercive control: proving a "course of behaviour" under s.1 of the Domestic Abuse (Scotland) Act 2018' (2020) 24 *International Journal of Evidence and Proof* 396; Forbes E.E., 'The Domestic Abuse (Scotland) Act 2018: the whole story?' (2018) 22 *Edinburgh Law Review* 406; Cairns I., 'What counts as "domestic"? Family relationships and the proposed criminalization of domestic abuse in Scotland' (2017) 21 *Edinburgh Law Review* 262; and Hughes M., 'The Domestic Abuse (Scotland) Act 2018: a general guide and civil ramifications' (2019) 20 *Scots Law Times* 59.

enacted in Northern Ireland under section 1 of the Domestic Abuse and Civil Proceedings Act (Northern Ireland) 2021.[23]

The way in which domestic abuse has been conceptualised by the ECtHR has also evolved, as will be discussed further in Chapter 2. As with domestic legislators in the UK, the ECtHR has likewise recognised the concept of coercive control.[24] In addition, in its early jurisprudence on domestic abuse, the Court largely framed such abuse as a violation of Article 8 of the ECHR; however, the ECtHR now conceptualises domestic abuse much more frequently as a breach of Article 3.

Furthermore, questions relating to gender and domestic abuse have raised a great deal of debate. It is, of course, accepted that both women and men can be victims of domestic abuse and that both women and men can be perpetrators of such abuse. For example, the legislative provisions addressing domestic abuse, which have been enacted in the various jurisdictions in the UK, as referred to above, all adopt a gender-neutral approach, and correctly so. However, as Burton remarks, 'Contradictory views about whether women are as likely as men to perpetrate violence against an intimate partner abound in the literature'.[25] Nevertheless, Dobash and Dobash are of the view that women's violence against men differs substantially from men's violence against women in terms of the context and the consequences.[26] Women's violence often takes place in the context of self-defence and the consequences of women's violence against men are less severe. Essentially, 'Women's violence towards male intimate partners does not occur with the same frequency or ferocity as men's violence towards female intimate partners'.[27] Dobash and Dobash are thus of the view that in formulating policies, priority should be accorded to those which tackle men's violence against women.[28] Likewise, Chinkin comments that, 'while men also experience domestic violence, it is more frequently inflicted upon women and has disparate economic and social consequences'.[29] Kimmell goes so far as to state that, 'When sexual violence and violence by ex-spouses are considered, the evidence is overwhelming that

23 For a discussion of the Domestic Abuse and Civil Proceedings Act (Northern Ireland) 2021, see McQuigg R., *Criminal Justice Responses to Domestic Abuse in Northern Ireland*, 2022, Routledge, Abingdon, at 80–97; and Bettinson V. and McQuigg R. (eds), *Criminalising Coercive Control: Challenges for the Implementation of Northern Ireland's Domestic Abuse Offence*, 2023, Routledge, Abingdon.

24 See *Volodina v. Russia* (App. No. 41261/17), judgment of 9 July 2019, at para. 75.

25 Burton M., *Legal Responses to Domestic Violence*, 2008, Routledge-Cavendish, Abingdon, at 5.

26 Dobash R.P. and Dobash R.E., 'Women's Violence to Men in Intimate Relationships: Working on a Puzzle' (2004) 44 *British Journal of Criminology*, 324–349.

27 Burton, op. cit., at 6.

28 Dobash and Dobash, op. cit.

29 Chinkin C., 'Addressing violence against women in the Commonwealth within states' obligations under international law' (2014) 40 *Commonwealth Law Bulletin* 471 at 475.

gender asymmetry in domestic violence remains in full effect'.[30] Domestic abuse has long been viewed by UN bodies such as the CEDAW Committee as constituting a form of discrimination against women. Indeed, as Chinkin comments, the CEDAW Committee has rejected the view that domestic abuse 'can be described in gender-neutral language that conceals the gender-based quality of violence against women'.[31] Likewise, as will be explored in Chapter 3, there has also been a growing recognition on the part of the ECtHR of domestic abuse as a form of gender-based discrimination.

International Human Rights Law and Domestic Abuse

As noted above, it is only relatively recently that domestic abuse began to be regarded as an issue for international human rights law.[32] The main problem in this respect lay in the manner in which rights were formulated. As Thomas and Beasley state, 'The concept of human rights developed largely from Western political theory of the rights of the individual to autonomy and freedom'.[33] The foundation of international relations is the idea of the liberal state. As Romany remarks, 'Liberalism constructs a social and political order which seeks to emancipate the individual from the oppression of political structures'.[34] International law therefore has its basis in the liberal social contract theory, whereby states are viewed as individuals which should have independence, freedom and equality. Inherent to this theory is the concept of negative rights ensuring individual freedom. This idea is thus deeply embedded in the discourse of international law, and consequently human rights

30 Kimmel M.S., '"Gender Symmetry" in Domestic Violence: A Substantive and Methodological Research Review' (2002) 6 *Violence Against Women*, 1332–1363 at 1359. For further discussion of arguments surrounding 'gender symmetry' regarding domestic abuse, see Johnson M.P., 'Conflict and Control: Gender Symmetry and Asymmetry in Domestic Violence' (2006) 12 *Violence Against Women* 1003.

31 Chinkin C., 'Violence Against Women' in Freeman M.A., Chinkin C. and Rudolf B. (eds), *The UN Convention on the Elimination of All Forms of Discrimination Against Women – A Commentary*, 2012, Oxford University Press, Oxford, 443 at 452.

32 For further discussion of domestic abuse as an issue for international human rights law, see McQuigg R., *The Istanbul Convention, Domestic Violence and Human Rights*, 2017, Routledge, Abingdon, 17–31; McQuigg R., *International Human Rights Law and Domestic Violence*, 2011, Routledge, Abingdon, 3–8 and 78–98; McQuigg R., *Criminal Justice Responses to Domestic Abuse in Northern Ireland*, 2022, Routledge, Abingdon, 21–36; Meyersfeld B., *Domestic Violence and International Law*, 2010, Hart Publishing, Oxford, 24–78; and Hesselbacher L., 'State Obligations regarding Domestic Violence: The European Court of Human Rights, Due Diligence, and International Legal Minimums of Protection' (2010) 8 *Northwestern Journal of International Human Rights* 190 at 191–200.

33 Thomas D.Q. and Beasley M.E., 'Symposium on Reconceptualizing Violence Against Women by Intimate Partners' (1995) 58 *Albany Law Review* 1119 at 1121.

34 Romany C., 'Women as Aliens: A Feminist Critique of the Public/Private Distinction in International Human Rights Law' (1993) 6 *Harvard Human Rights Journal* 87 at 90.

law.[35] Essentially the concept of 'negative rights' entails that the state cannot interfere with an individual in particular aspects of his or her life.[36]

The concept of negative rights ensuring individual freedoms emerged again during the fight against totalitarianism, which was a catalyst in the development of human rights law. As Fredman remarks, 'Human rights have long been understood as providing protection for individual freedom against an intrusive State'.[37] As Thomas and Beasley comment, 'States are bound by international law to respect the individual rights of each and every person and are thus accountable for abuses of those rights'.[38] However, the rights norms that emerged were generally formulated in a very negative manner, whereby the state was required only to refrain from breaching the rights in question. There were no duties on the state to take positive steps to ensure that the rights of the individual were not violated. As Romany comments, the ultimate concern was the separation and protection of the individual from the state.[39] The objective of the framers of the earlier human rights instruments was to ensure that there was a space wherein the individual would be 'left alone' by the state. Their aim was not to obtain positive entitlements from the state. Rights thus developed in such a way as to create a public/private dichotomy by which human rights norms were upheld in the public sphere where the state was involved, but were not applied in the private sphere.

As Burton comments, 'In the classic public/private dichotomy intimate relationships are seen as part of the "private" sphere not suitable for public regulation'.[40] Indeed, as Ewing remarks, 'The public/private distinction in international law … places many forms of violence against women beyond the protective scope of human rights instruments'.[41] The rights of women

35 Romany, op. cit., at 89–98.

36 For historical arguments on rights, see Harvey C., 'Talking about Human Rights' (2004) *European Human Rights Law Review* 500.

37 Fredman S., *Human Rights Transformed – Positive Rights and Positive Duties*, 2009, Oxford University Press, Oxford, at 1. See also Hirschl R., '"Negative" Rights vs. "Positive" Entitlements: A Comparative Study of Judicial Interpretations of Rights in an Emerging Neo-Liberal Economic Order' (2000) 22 *Human Rights Quarterly* 1060.

38 Thomas and Beasley, op. cit., at 121.

39 Romany C., 'State Responsibility Goes Private: A Feminist Critique of the Public/Private Distinction in International Human Rights Law', in Cook R.J. (ed.), *Human Rights of Women – National and International Perspectives*, 1994, University of Pennsylvania Press, Philadelphia, 85 at 89.

40 Burton M., op. cit., at 7. See also Lacey N., *Unspeakable Subjects*, 1998, Hart Publishing, Oxford, at 71–97; Romany C., 'Women as Aliens: A Feminist Critique of the Public/Private Distinction in International Human Rights Law' (1993) 6 *Harvard Human Rights Journal* 87; and Cook R.J., 'Women's International Human Rights Law: The Way Forward', in Cook R.J. (ed.), *Human Rights of Women – National and International Perspectives*, 1994, University of Pennsylvania Press, Pennsylvania, 3 at 3.

41 Ewing A.P., 'Establishing State Responsibility For Private Acts of Violence Against Women Under the American Convention on Human Rights' (1995) 26 *Columbia Human Rights Law Review* 751 at 753.

often come into conflict with powers other than that of the state. These powers generally emanate from the private arena, such as from within the family unit.[42] Knop states that 'women are more vulnerable than men to serious harm, injustice, and discrimination in the private sphere, and the public/private distinction has prevented the law from remedying the situation'.[43] Women all around the globe suffer from violence occurring in the private sphere, such as domestic abuse, female genital mutilation and dowry killing.[44] Under traditional principles, such abuses did not come within the scope of human rights law as they are not inflicted directly by the state. As Isa remarks, 'international human rights law and the set of international legal norms it encompasses has developed in such a way that it reflects the experiences of men, excluding those of women'.[45] Van Leeuwen comments that 'abuses, exclusions and constraints that are more typical of women's lives are neither recognised nor protected by mainstream human rights instruments'.[46] Charlesworth states that the main impact of the public/private dichotomy has been 'to muffle, and often completely silence, the voices of women'.[47]

Nevertheless, the public/private divide does not now pose an intractable problem for the recognition of domestic abuse as an issue for international human rights law. The doctrine of state responsibility has been developed, under which positive obligations can be placed on the state to ensure that human rights standards are upheld in situations involving only private individuals. An increasingly expansive reading of human rights strengthens the role of this body of law in protecting individuals. For instance, the UN human rights bodies often refer to the state's duties to respect, protect, promote and fulfil rights.

Although none of the UN human rights treaties make any express reference to domestic abuse,[48] in 1992 the CEDAW Committee issued General Recommendation No. 19 which interpreted CEDAW as prohibiting violence

42 Rishmawi M., 'The Developing Approaches of the International Commission of Jurists to Women's Human Rights', in Cook R.J. (ed.), *Human Rights of Women – National and International Perspectives*, 1994, University of Pennsylvania Press, Philadelphia, 340 at 341.

43 Knop K., 'Introduction', in Knop K. (ed.), *Gender and Human Rights*, 2004, Oxford University Press, Oxford, 1 at 6.

44 Rishmawi, op. cit., at 341.

45 Isa F.G., 'The Optional Protocol for the Convention on the Elimination of All Forms of Discrimination Against Women: Strengthening the Protection of Women's Human Rights' (2003) 20 *Arizona Journal of International and Comparative Law* 291 at 293.

46 Van Leeuwen F., *Women's Rights Are Human Rights*, 2010, Intersentia, Antwerp, at p. 9.

47 Charlesworth H., 'What are 'Women's International Human Rights'?', in Cook, R.J. (ed.), *Human Rights of Women – National and International Perspectives*, 1994, University of Pennsylvania Press, Philadelphia, 58 at 68.

48 For a discussion of whether treaty provisions on violence against women should be adopted at the UN level, see McQuigg R., 'Is it time for a UN Treaty on Violence against Women?' (2018) 22 *International Journal of Human Rights* 305.

against women in both the public and private spheres. General Recommendation No. 19 stated that, 'The full implementation of the Convention required States to take positive measures to eliminate all forms of violence against women'.[49] The General Recommendation then asserted that,

> The definition of discrimination includes gender-based violence, that is, violence that is directed against a woman because she is a woman or that affects women disproportionately. It includes acts that inflict physical, mental or sexual harm or suffering, threats of such acts, coercion and other deprivations of liberty. Gender-based violence may breach specific provisions of the Convention, regardless of whether those provisions expressly mention violence.[50]

The General Recommendation stated that gender-based violence may breach *inter alia* the right to life; the right not to be subject to torture or to cruel, inhuman or degrading treatment or punishment; and the right to liberty and security of person.[51] It asserted that,

> discrimination under the Convention is not restricted to action by or on behalf of Governments ... Under general international law and specific human rights covenants, States may be responsible for private acts if they fail to act with due diligence to prevent violations of rights or to investigate and punish acts of violence, and for providing compensation.[52]

The General Recommendation also emphasised that,

> Family violence is one of the most insidious forms of violence against women. It is prevalent in all societies. Within family relationships women of all ages are subjected to violence of all kinds, including battering, rape, other forms of sexual assault, mental and other forms of violence, which are perpetuated by traditional attitudes.[53]

More recently, in 2017, the CEDAW Committee issued General Recommendation No. 35 on gender-based violence against women, the

49 UN Committee on the Elimination of Discrimination Against Women, 'General Recommendation No. 19: Violence against women' (1992), para. 4.

50 Para. 6.

51 Para. 7.

52 Para. 9.

53 Para. 23.

purpose of which was essentially to update General Recommendation No. 19.[54]

In 1993, the UN General Assembly issued the UN Declaration on the Elimination of Violence against Women,[55] which stressed the need to address the issue of domestic abuse in order to protect the right to life; the right not to be subjected to torture or other cruel, inhuman or degrading treatment or punishment; the right to equality; the right to liberty and security of person; the right to equal protection under the law; the right to be free from all forms of discrimination; and the right to the highest standard attainable of physical and mental health.[56] Following the World Conference on Human Rights, which was held in Vienna in 1993,[57] a Special Rapporteur on violence against women, its causes and consequences, was appointed by the UN Commission on Human Rights. It has been commented that the Special Rapporteur 'brought international consciousness to a new level'.[58] The first holder of the post, Radhika Coomaraswamy, was appointed in 1994, and in 1996 she produced a framework for model legislation on domestic violence.[59] The Fourth World Conference on Women was held in 1995 in Beijing, with the resulting Platform for Action urging states to adopt a wide range of measures regarding violence against women.[60] In addition, the UN Commission on Human Rights and the Human Rights Council which succeeded it, have also issued statements relevant to domestic abuse.[61]

Overall, various categories of recommendations have been made to states by the UN bodies in terms of responding to domestic abuse. These include the adoption of measures relating to improving their criminal justice systems; improving measures of civil protection; providing social support measures for victims; increasing awareness within society of issues surrounding domestic abuse; increasing awareness of professionals who may be particularly likely

54 UN Committee on the Elimination of Discrimination Against Women, 'General recommendation No. 35 on gender-based violence against women, updating general recommendation No. 19' (2017). For further discussion of General Recommendation No. 35, see McQuigg R., 'The CEDAW Committee and Gender-Based Violence against Women: General Recommendation No 35' (2017) 6 *International Human Rights Law Review* 263.

55 Declaration on the Elimination of Violence against Women, General Assembly Resolution 48/104 (20 December 1993).

56 Article 3.

57 United Nations, 'Vienna Declaration and Programme of Action' (25 June 1993).

58 Stark B., 'Symposium on Integrating Responses to Domestic Violence' (2001) 47 *Loyola Law Review* 255 at 265.

59 Report of the Special Rapporteur on violence against women, its causes and consequences – A framework for model legislation on domestic violence, E/CN.4/1996/53/Add.2 (2 February 1996).

60 Beijing Platform for Action, U.N. Doc.A/CONF.177/20 (1995).

61 See, for example, Commission on Human Rights Resolution 2001/49 (23 April 2001); Commission on Human Rights Resolution 2004/46, 20 April 2004; and Human Rights Council Resolution 14/12 (30 June 2010).

to come into contact with victims; and developing programmes for perpetrators. In addition, the CEDAW Committee has now considered a number of complaints in relation to the responses of states to domestic abuse which have been taken under the Optional Protocol procedure,[62] which enables individuals or groups to submit to the Committee claims of breaches of CEDAW.

The growing recognition of domestic abuse as an issue for human rights law is not confined to the UN system. In 1994, the Inter-American Convention on the Prevention, Punishment and Eradication of Violence against Women (Convention of Belém do Pará) was adopted by the General Assembly of the Organization of American States.[63] In addition, the Protocol to the African Charter on Human and Peoples' Rights on the Rights of Women in Africa (Maputo Protocol), which encompasses *inter alia* violence against women, was adopted by the African Union in 2003;[64] and in 2011 the Council of Europe adopted the Istanbul Convention.[65] Also, the ECtHR has developed a considerable body of jurisprudence which directly addresses the issue of domestic abuse through the use of the doctrine of positive obligations.

The ECHR and the Doctrine of Positive Obligations

The ECHR was opened for signature in November 1950 and came into force in September 1953.

This instrument 'arose out of the determination of the signatory States to consign to history the atrocities of the Second World War',[66] and most of its provisions are framed in a negative way with the emphasis being placed on the state's duty of non-interference. As Schriver asserts, 'The express provisions of the Convention do not require the European Court to impose

62 See, for example, *AT v. Hungary* (Communication No. 2/2003, 26 January 2005, CEDAW/C/32/D/2/2003); *Goekce v. Austria* (Communication No. 5/2005, 6 August 2007, CEDAW/C/39/D/5/2005); *Yildirim v. Austria* (Communication No. 6/2005, 1 October 2007, CEDAW/C/39/D/6/2005); *VK v. Bulgaria* (Communication No. 20/2008, 17 August 2011, CEDAW/C/49/D/20/2008); and *Jallow v. Bulgaria* (Communication No. 32/2011, 28 August 2012, CEDAW/C/52/D/32/2011).

63 For a discussion of the Convention of Belém do Pará, see McQuigg (2017), *The Istanbul Convention, Domestic Violence and Human Rights*, op. cit., at 31–33.

64 For a discussion of the Maputo Protocol, see McQuigg (2017), *The Istanbul Convention, Domestic Violence and Human Rights*, op. cit., at 33–35.

65 For a discussion of the Istanbul Convention, see McQuigg (2017), *The Istanbul Convention, Domestic Violence and Human Rights*, op. cit.; McQuigg R., 'What Potential does the Council of Europe Convention on Violence against Women hold as regards Domestic Violence?' (2012) 16 *International Journal of Human Rights* 947; and McQuigg R., 'A Contextual Analysis of the Council of Europe's Convention on Preventing and Combating Violence against Women' (2012) 1 *International Human Rights Law Review* 367.

66 Council of Europe, 'The European Convention on Human Rights – A Living Instrument', September 2022, https://echr.coe.int/Documents/Convention_Instrument_ENG.pdf, at 9.

affirmative duties'.[67] Indeed, the ECHR provides a very clear example of the negative formulation of rights that is found in many human rights instruments, as discussed above.

However, in certain instances, positive duties can be placed on states to protect the rights of individuals from threats posed by other private entities.[68] The ECtHR has derived this principle from three propositions. Firstly, under Article 1 of the ECHR, states must secure the rights of everyone within their jurisdictions. This appears to indicate that states must take positive steps to ensure that private individuals can freely enjoy their rights. Secondly, it is assumed that rights must be effective and not merely theoretical.[69] As Clapham remarks, 'an "effective" implementation of the Convention means that the changing social context within which it operates has to be considered'.[70] It is being increasingly recognised that violations of rights may emanate from the private sphere just as easily as they can be perpetrated by the state itself. States are subject to international human rights law and to public disapproval if they violate its terms. However, individuals are not subjected to such controls and it is thus likely that more human rights abuses take place in the private sphere than in the public arena. In order to reflect this social reality, the ECtHR realises that duties must be placed on states to protect the human rights of individuals from threats posed by other individuals. As Mowbray comments, 'Passive non-interference by governmental authorities with persons' Convention rights is not sufficient to ensure that many of those rights are fully and effectively respected'.[71] Thirdly, under Article 13, states must provide effective remedies for breaches of rights.[72] Again, this provision serves to impose positive duties on states.

Nevertheless, it could be argued that the ECtHR has built, and is continuing to build, an extremely important body of jurisprudence on a rather unstable foundation. The reference in Article 1 of the ECHR to securing rights, and the Article 13 right to a remedy are more than balanced out by the generally negative framework of rights which forms the remainder of this instrument. The principle of effectiveness is simply a judge-made assumption. However, it is clear that the correct course has been adopted. The ECtHR generally takes

67 Schriver T., 'Establishing an Affirmative Governmental Duty to Protect Children's Rights: The European Court of Human Rights as a Model for the United States Supreme Court' (2000) 34 *University of San Francisco Law Review*, 379–408 at 400.

68 For further discussion of the doctrine of positive obligations, see McQuigg (2011), op. cit., at 43–46.

69 Starmer K., *European Human Rights Law, the Human Rights Act 1998 and the European Convention on Human Rights*, 1999, LAG, London, at 194.

70 Clapham A., *Human Rights in the Private Sphere*, 1993, Clarendon Press, Oxford, at 178.

71 Mowbray A.R., *The Development of Positive Obligations under the European Convention on Human Rights by the European Court of Human Rights*, 2004, Hart Publishing, Oxford, at 221.

72 Starmer, op. cit., at 194.

a teleological approach to the interpretation of the ECHR, wherein it looks beyond the actual wording of the text to the purpose for which this instrument was created. As Schriver comments, 'By adopting this dynamic system of interpretation, the European Court has expanded on the broad language of Convention rights and ensured full protection to the individual in the face of changes in European political and social attitudes'.[73] The ECtHR goes beyond the original intentions of those who drafted the ECHR and takes account of contemporary standards.[74] The 'forward-looking and contextual'[75] approach of the ECtHR, 'effectively moves all the Member States toward human rights reforms'.[76]

The positive obligations which may be placed on states are wide ranging. Notably, Starmer claims that the ECtHR has recognised five main categories of such obligations that can be imposed on states – a duty to establish a legal framework providing effective rights protection, an obligation to prevent violations of ECHR rights, a duty to provide information relevant to the breach of ECHR rights, an obligation to respond to violations and a duty to provide resources to individuals to prevent breaches of their rights.[77] With regard to the final category of obligations identified by Starmer, it must be noted that the rights contained in the ECHR largely fall within the category of 'civil and political' rights, as opposed to 'socioeconomic' rights.[78] It is arguable that this instrument is therefore less than ideal in terms of addressing domestic abuse, given that, as Schneider comments, the most pressing needs of victims of such abuse may be to receive social support measures, such as refuge accommodation, monetary resources and housing.[79] It is certainly true that, until very recently, the jurisprudence of the ECtHR on domestic abuse has focused almost exclusively on issues surrounding criminal justice responses to such abuse. Nevertheless, the Court has now shown itself to be willing to apply ECHR provisions to other issues relating to state responses to domestic abuse, as are considered in Chapters 3 and 5.

73 Schriver, op. cit., at 399.

74 Schriver, op. cit., at 401.

75 Clapham, op. cit., at 178.

76 Schriver, op. cit., at 402.

77 Starmer, op. cit., at 196.

78 For further discussion, see Koch I.E., Human Rights as Indivisible Rights: The Protection of Socio-economic Demands under the European Convention on Human Rights, 2009, Martinus Nijhoff Publishers, Leiden.

79 Schneider E.M., *Battered Women and Feminist Lawmaking*, 2000, Yale University Press, London, at 196–197.

Chapter Outline

Chapter 2 explores the theme of how conceptualisations of domestic abuse in the jurisprudence of the ECtHR have evolved. In the Court's early case law on this issue, its approach to the use of Articles 3 and 8 was somewhat incoherent, in terms of on which provision it based its findings of violations of the ECHR. Essentially, the ECtHR seemed to take the view that if a breach was found, it did not matter to any great extent whether the abuse in question was conceptualised as a violation of Article 3 or Article 8. It is likely that the Court's apparent preference for the use of Article 8 as opposed to Article 3 in its earlier jurisprudence on domestic abuse was due simply to the fact that it can be more straightforward to establish a violation of Article 8 than it is to establish a breach of Article 3. However, in *Valiuliene v. Lithuania*,[80] the state argued that the ill-treatment to which the applicant, a victim of domestic abuse, had been subjected had not been sufficiently severe to fall within the ambit of Article 3, and the state presented the ECtHR with a unilateral declaration acknowledging a breach of Article 8. The Court refused to accept this declaration, found a violation of Article 3 and stated that it was not necessary to examine the complaint under Article 8, as a breach of Article 3 had already been found. It seems that the case of *Valiuliene* served to highlight to the ECtHR that an important issue in domestic abuse cases is not only whether a violation of the ECHR is found, but also on which provision such a finding is based. Indeed, this case marked a change in the Court's approach and henceforth Article 3 was used much more extensively in such cases. It is also notable that the ECtHR has recognised a conceptualisation of domestic abuse as 'coercive control'.

However, the book argues that although conceptualisations of domestic abuse in the case law of the ECtHR have evolved greatly in a very meritorious manner, further development of the Court's conceptualisation of this issue is still needed. As is also examined in Chapter 2, despite the fact that it has now been firmly established that domestic abuse falls within the scope of Article 3, the ECtHR has not yet expressly found in any case involving domestic abuse that such abuse violates the 'torture' limb of this provision, as distinguished from 'inhuman or degrading treatment'. In *Volodina v. Russia*[81] and *Tunikova and Others v. Russia*,[82] both of which involved domestic abuse, questions arose as to whether the Court should have expressly found violations of the 'torture' limb of Article 3, and the chapter includes discussion of the potential merits of such a finding in a domestic abuse case.

Chapter 3 develops the theme of the ECtHR's evolving conceptualisation of domestic abuse – by focusing on a further facet of this – namely the

80 (App. No. 33234/07), judgment of 26 March 2013.
81 (App. No. 41261/17), judgment of 9 July 2019.
82 (App. Nos. 55974/16, 53118/17, 27484/18, 28011/19), judgment of 14 December 2021.

Court's approach to domestic abuse as a form of gender-based discrimination under Article 14. The use of this provision in such cases has expanded greatly in recent years, which is reflective of the increased use of Article 14 by the ECtHR generally. The Court has very clearly framed domestic abuse as a form of gender-based discrimination, as is discussed in this chapter. Also, despite the fact that the ECtHR's jurisprudence on domestic abuse focuses to a very large extent on criminal justice responses to such abuse, it is noteworthy that the Court has now applied Article 14 in a case relating to housing in a domestic abuse context.[83] It is argued that the willingness of the ECtHR to address matters regarding state responses to domestic abuse beyond those relating to criminal justice is meritorious, and that the Court should continue to adopt such an approach.

A prominent theme in this book is the development of the ECtHR's understanding of domestic abuse. Chapter 4 analyses an important issue which has arisen in this regard – namely the question of how the '*Osman* test' should be applied in the context of domestic abuse. This test is derived from the judgment of the ECtHR in *Osman v. United Kingdom*[84] and is applied by the Court in all cases in which it is alleged that a state has failed to take appropriate steps to protect the right to life of an individual from the criminal acts of a third party. In *Osman* it was established that in appropriate circumstances Article 2 entails a positive duty on the state to take preventive operational measures to protect an individual whose life is at risk from the criminal acts of another individual. Nevertheless, for such a positive duty to arise,

> it must be established that the authorities knew or ought to have known at the time of the existence of a real and immediate risk to the life of an identified individual from the criminal acts of a third party and that they failed to take measures within the scope of their powers which, judged reasonably, might have been expected to avoid that risk.[85]

However, a recognition began to grow within the ECtHR that the application of the *Osman* test in circumstances involving domestic abuse could be problematic in terms of the need for the authorities to be aware of an 'immediate' risk to life in order for a positive duty to take preventive operational measures to arise.[86] In the context of domestic abuse, even if a risk to life does not

83 *J.D. and A v. United Kingdom*, (App. Nos. 32949/17, 34614/17), judgment of 24 October 2019.
84 (App. No. 23452/94), judgment of 28 October 1998.
85 At para. 116.
86 See, for example, *Valiuliene v. Lithuania* (App. No. 33234/07), judgment of 26 March 2013, Concurring Opinion of Judge Pinto de Albuquerque, at para. 31; *Volodina v. Russia* (App. No. 41261/17), judgment of 9 July 2019, Separate Opinion of Judge Pinto de Albuquerque, joined by Judge Dedov, at para. 12; and *Kurt v. Austria* (App. No. 62903/15), judgment of 4 July 2019 (first instance judgment), Concurring Opinion of Judge Huseynov, at paras. 3–4.

appear to be immediate as such, there is a substantial possibility that this could escalate at any point.

The importance of this issue was such that it became the focus of the first Grand Chamber judgment in a domestic abuse case. In its June 2021 judgment in *Kurt v. Austria*,[87] the Grand Chamber established that the 'immediacy' element of the *Osman* test should be interpreted in such a manner as to take account of the specific nature of domestic abuse. Chapter 4 includes detailed discussion of the Grand Chamber's judgment and of how the principles established therein have subsequently been applied by the ECtHR.[88] It is argued that the judgment constitutes a landmark in the Court's jurisprudence on domestic abuse, and in particular as regards the use of Article 2 in such cases. The Grand Chamber settled the questions which had arisen regarding how the *Osman* test should be applied in cases involving domestic abuse and indeed whether it should be used at all in such cases. It is now beyond doubt that, although the *Osman* test should be used, it must be applied in such a manner as to take account of the specific circumstances of domestic abuse. This is a welcome recognition, which demonstrates how the ECtHR's understanding of domestic abuse has increased and developed. However, it is also argued that the way in which the majority of the Grand Chamber proceeded to apply the very meritorious principles articulated in the first part of the judgment to the specific facts of the case in question is problematic. Having established that account must be taken of the particular circumstances of domestic abuse, it seems that the majority may then have failed to take these circumstances into consideration in a sufficient manner.

Chapter 5 focuses on a number of issues that have arisen in the ECtHR's very recent jurisprudence on domestic abuse, which have been addressed by the Court using Article 8. As noted above, Article 8 was used more extensively in the Court's earlier jurisprudence on domestic abuse.[89] However, the ECtHR has found violations of Article 8 in the recent cases of *Buturugă v. Romania*[90] and *Volodina v. Russia (No. 2)*,[91] both of which involved the very current issue of cyberviolence. In recent times, there has been a growing recognition of the ways in which perpetrators may use technology in their abuse, and Chapter 5 considers the Court's approach to this issue. Also, as noted

87 (App. No. 62903/15), judgment of 15 June 2021.

88 Relevant cases include *Tkhelidze v. Georgia* (App. No. 33056/17), judgment of 8 July 2021; Y *and Others v. Bulgaria* (App. No. 9077/18), judgment of 22 March 2022; and *Landi v. Italy* (App. No. 10929/19), judgment of 7 April 2022.

89 For example, *Bevacqua and S v. Bulgaria* (App. No. 71127/01), judgment of 12 June 2008; *A v. Croatia* (App. No. 55164/08), judgment of 14 October 2010; and *Kalucza v. Hungary* (App. No. 57693/10), judgment of 24 April 2012.

90 (App. No. 56867/15), judgment of 11 February 2020. A violation of Article 3 was also found in this case.

91 (App. No. 40419/19), judgment of 14 September 2021.

above, while the ECtHR's early case law on domestic abuse focused almost exclusively on the responses of criminal justice systems, this body of jurisprudence has now evolved to encompass other aspects of state responses to such abuse. For example, in *Levchuk v. Ukraine*[92] a breach of Article 8 was found in circumstances in which a victim of domestic abuse complained that the domestic courts had refused to order the eviction of her former husband from a flat that they occupied. Likewise, violations of Article 8 were found in *I.M. and Others v. Italy*[93] and *Luca v. Moldova*,[94] both of which related to issues surrounding child contact in the context of domestic abuse. Given that the early case law of the ECtHR on domestic abuse focused almost exclusively on the responses of police and prosecutors, it is argued that the fact that this body of jurisprudence has now reached a stage whereby it encompasses detailed consideration of a specific issue such as child contact demonstrates the extent to which the Court's understanding of domestic abuse has developed.

Chapter 6 summarises the key points and conclusions from the preceding discussion. A considerable body of important jurisprudence on the issue of domestic abuse has certainly been developed by the ECtHR within a relatively short space of time. The ways in which the Court has conceptualised domestic abuse have evolved and are likely to develop further in the future. In particular, such abuse may be expressly conceptualised by the ECtHR as torture, a development that would serve to emphasise the seriousness of this issue. Likewise, it is argued that the Court's understanding of the dynamics of domestic abuse has developed, as epitomised by the recognition by the Grand Chamber in *Kurt v. Austria* that the *Osman* test must be applied in cases involving domestic abuse in such a manner as to take account of the particular context of such abuse. The ECtHR has also demonstrated a willingness to develop its jurisprudence on domestic abuse beyond exclusively addressing issues relating to criminal justice responses, and it is argued that the Court should continue to expand this approach, particularly as the primary needs of victims may be for social support measures. Overall, the ECtHR is to be commended for its willingness to develop its approaches to domestic abuse, and it remains to be seen how the Court's jurisprudence on this issue will evolve further in the future.

92 (App. No. 17496/19), judgment of 3 September 2020.
93 (App. No. 25426/20), judgment of 10 November 2022.
94 (App. No. 55351/17), judgment of 17 October 2023.

2 Conceptualising Domestic Abuse

Chapter 2 explores the theme of how conceptualisations of domestic abuse in the jurisprudence of the ECtHR have evolved. In the Court's early jurisprudence, its approach to the use of Article 3 (the right to be free from torture or inhuman or degrading treatment) and Article 8 (the right to respect for one's private and family life) in domestic abuse cases was somewhat incoherent, in terms of on which provision the Court based its findings of violations of the ECHR. Essentially the ECtHR seemed to take the view that if a breach was found, it did not matter to any great extent whether the abuse in question was conceptualised as a violation of Article 3 or Article 8. However, the case of *Valiuliene v. Lithuania*,[1] marked a change in the Court's approach, as is discussed in this chapter, and henceforth Article 3 was used much more extensively in domestic abuse cases. Importantly, the ECtHR has also recognised a conceptualisation of domestic abuse as 'coercive control'.

However, it is argued that although conceptualisations of domestic abuse in the case law of the ECtHR have evolved greatly in a very meritorious manner, further development of the Court's conceptualisation of this issue is still needed. Despite the fact that it has now been firmly established that domestic abuse falls within the scope of Article 3, the Court has not yet expressly found that such abuse violates the 'torture' limb of this provision, as distinguished from 'inhuman or degrading treatment'. In *Volodina v. Russia*[2] and *Tunikova and Others v. Russia*,[3] both of which involved domestic abuse, questions arose as to whether the ECtHR should have expressly found violations of the 'torture' limb of Article 3, and the chapter includes a discussion of the potential merits of such a finding in a domestic abuse case.

1 (App. No. 33234/07), judgment of 26 March 2013.
2 (App. No. 41261/17), judgment of 9 July 2019.
3 (App. Nos. 55974/16, 53118/17, 27484/18, 28011/19), judgment of 14 December 2021.

DOI: 10.4324/9781003493068-2

Early Conceptualisations of Domestic Abuse

In its early jurisprudence on domestic abuse, the approach of the ECtHR in terms of conceptualising domestic abuse as a violation of Article 3 or as a breach of Article 8 tended to be somewhat inconsistent and incoherent. Writing in 2006, prior to the inception of the jurisprudence of the ECtHR on domestic abuse, Choudhry and Herring correctly remarked that, 'Domestic violence will often be sufficiently intense to engage article 3'.[4] The ECtHR first found a breach of Article 3 in a domestic abuse case in its judgment of September 2009 in *Opuz v. Turkey*.[5] In this instance the applicant alleged that the authorities had failed to protect her and her mother from domestic abuse, which had resulted in the death of her mother and her own ill-treatment. The ECtHR found that the state authorities had failed to safeguard the right to life of the applicant's mother in violation of Article 2 of the ECHR. The applicant alleged that she herself had been subjected by her husband to violence, injury and death threats and that the authorities had been negligent towards her situation, which caused her pain and fear in violation of Article 3. She argued that the injuries she had suffered amounted to torture within the meaning of this provision. The ECtHR held that the violence suffered was sufficiently serious to amount to ill-treatment within the meaning of Article 3, although it did not specify whether it amounted to torture, as opposed to inhuman or degrading treatment. The Court concluded that there had been a violation of Article 3 'as a result of the State authorities' failure to take protective measures in the form of effective deterrence against serious breaches of the applicant's personal integrity by her husband'.[6]

Opuz v. Turkey represented a crucial step in the jurisprudence of the ECtHR in this area, in that it had now been held that domestic abuse could constitute a violation of Article 3. Three months after its judgment in *Opuz*, the ECtHR found a breach of Article 3 in another domestic abuse case, that of *E.S. and Others v. Slovakia*.[7] However, equally, there were other cases involving domestic abuse, such as *Bevacqua and S v. Bulgaria*,[8] *A v. Croatia*[9] and

4 Choudhry S. and Herring J., 'Domestic Violence and the Human Rights Act 1998: A New Means of Legal Intervention?' (2006) *Public Law* 752 at 759.

5 (App. No. 33401/02), judgment of 9 September 2009. For further discussion of this case, see Burton M., 'The human rights of victims of domestic violence: *Opuz v. Turkey*' (2010) 22 *Child and Family Law Quarterly* 131; and Londono P., 'Developing Human Rights Principles in Cases of Gender-Based Violence: *Opuz v. Turkey* in the European Court of Human Rights' (2009) 9 *Human Rights Law Review* 662.

6 At para. 176. A violation of Article 14, the non-discrimination provision, was also found in this case.

7 (App. No. 8227/04), judgment of 15 December 2009. The Court also found a violation of Article 8 in this case.

8 (App. No. 71127/01), judgment of 12 September 2008.

9 (App. No. 55164/08), judgment of 14 October 2010.

Kalucza v. Hungary,[10] in which the ECtHR found violations of Article 8 only and refrained from also examining the cases under Article 3. The question arises therefore of why the Court adopted the latter approach in such cases.

There were at least two possible reasons for the Court's approach of finding violations of Article 8 and then omitting to consider Article 3 in certain cases involving domestic abuse. The first, and perhaps less charitable explanation, is that in the past the ECtHR may not have fully appreciated the seriousness of domestic abuse and therefore felt that it was more appropriate to conceptualise such abuse as a violation of the right to respect for private and family life, as opposed to a breach of the non-derogable right to be free from torture or inhuman or degrading treatment. However, it must be remembered that in certain relatively early cases, such as *Opuz v. Turkey*[11] and *E.S. and Others v. Slovakia*,[12] the Court did find violations of Article 3 in circumstances involving domestic abuse. It seems, therefore, that this explanation is less than satisfactory.

The second possible reason, and perhaps the more likely explanation for the Court's approach, relates purely to the issue of practicality. The ECtHR is burdened with a caseload which stretches its resources to breaking point and beyond. For instance, Mahoney refers to 'the regrettable inability of the European Court of Human Rights to process all cases in a timely manner'.[13] As Fraser remarks, the backlog of cases 'represents a structural and systemic problem for the Court'.[14] That being the situation, for reasons of expediency, the ECtHR frequently takes the approach of finding a violation of one provision of the ECHR and then omitting to consider the application of other provisions on which arguments have been made. This approach is adopted by the Court in many types of cases, and is by no means limited to the area of domestic abuse. The fact that in its early jurisprudence on such abuse, the ECtHR frequently seemed to display a preference for the use of Article 8 over that of Article 3 may simply have been due to the fact that it can be somewhat easier to establish a breach of Article 8 than it is to establish a violation of Article

10 (App. No. 57693/10), judgment of 24 April 2012.

11 (App. No. 33401/02).

12 (App. No. 8227/04).

13 Mahoney P., 'The European Court of Human Rights and its ever-growing caseload: Preserving the mission of the Court while ensuring the viability of the individual petition system' in Flogaitis S., Zwart T. and Fraser J. (eds), *The European Court of Human Rights and its Discontents – Turning Criticism into Strength*, 2013, Edward Elgar Publishing, Cheltenham, 18 at 18.

14 Fraser J., 'Conclusion: The European Convention on Human Rights as a common European endeavour' in Flogaitis S., Zwart T. and Fraser J. (eds), *The European Court of Human Rights and its Discontents – Turning Criticism into Strength*, 2013, Edward Elgar Publishing, Cheltenham, 192 at 194. See also Wildhaber L., 'Criticism and case-overload: Comments on the future of the European Court of Human Rights' in Flogaitis S., Zwart T. and Fraser J. (eds), *The European Court of Human Rights and its Discontents – Turning Criticism into Strength*, 2013, Edward Elgar Publishing, Cheltenham, 9.

3. If this was the reason behind the approach of the ECtHR, it is difficult to be unsympathetic to the Court, given the enormous pressure under which it works. Nevertheless, if the reason for the Court's approach was purely that of expediency, the difficulty was that such an approach risked being interpreted as an approach based on principle, with that principle being that domestic abuse was only serious enough to be conceptualised as a breach of Article 8, but did not in the majority of cases meet the threshold of constituting a violation of Article 3. This was problematic, to say the least, as was demonstrated in the case of *Valiuliene v. Lithuania*.

Valiuliene v. Lithuania: A Change in Approach

In *Valiuliene v. Lithuania*[15] the applicant argued that the state had failed to protect her sufficiently from domestic abuse and that the criminal proceedings she had instituted against her abuser had been futile. Between 3 January and 4 February 2001, the applicant had been beaten on five occasions by her partner, who was referred to in the judgment as J.H.L., with whom she had been living at the time. She alleged that she had been strangled, pulled by the hair, hit in the face, and kicked in the back and other parts of her body. On each occasion, forensic expert examinations had concluded that the injuries sustained by the applicant were minor and had not caused any health problems in the short or long term.

On 14 February 2001, the applicant lodged an application with the City District Court to bring a private prosecution against J.H.L., and in January 2002, the City District Court forwarded the applicant's complaint to the city public prosecutor, ordering him to start his own pre-trial criminal investigation. However, the investigation was suspended and reopened on numerous occasions due to J.H.L. failing to appear in court. In June 2005, the prosecutor decided to discontinue the pre-trial investigation on the grounds that, due to a change in the law in May 2003, the prosecution should have been brought by the applicant in a private capacity. The applicant appealed against this decision, pointing out that she had, in fact, initiated a private prosecution four years previously; however, the City District Court had transferred her complaint to a public prosecutor. The applicant argued that if the prosecutor had deemed that her case should be dealt with by means of a private prosecution, he should have informed her of this immediately after the new legislation had entered into force in May 2003 rather than waiting two years to inform her of his decision. This delay was particularly problematic as the end of the limitation period for prosecuting J.H.L. was fast approaching. However,

15 (App. No. 33234/07), judgment of 26 March 2013. For a discussion of this case, see also McQuigg R., 'The European Court of Human Rights and Domestic Violence: *Valiuliene v. Lithuania*' (2014) 18 *International Journal of Human Rights* 756.

the applicant's appeal was dismissed. The applicant subsequently attempted to bring a private prosecution against J.H.L.; however, her request was ultimately refused on the basis that the prosecution had now become time-barred.

Following the failure of her attempts to have J.H.L. prosecuted under domestic law, the applicant then brought a case to the ECtHR. Initially relying on Article 6 of the ECHR, the right to a fair trial, and Article 13, the right to an effective remedy, she argued that the national authorities had failed to investigate the acts of domestic abuse against her and to hold J.H.L. accountable. She also alleged that the criminal proceedings had been excessively lengthy. The ECtHR found, however, that the appropriate provisions to be relied upon in this instance were in fact Articles 3 and 8.

In response, the state asserted that the treatment to which the applicant had been subjected had not attained the minimum level of severity to fall within the scope of Article 3. The state argued that as the applicant had sustained minor bodily harm, which had not resulted in short or long-term health problems, 'it could be said that the injuries sustained by the applicant had been of a merely trivial nature'.[16] The state was of the view that responses to the ill-treatment other than relying on the criminal law could have been utilised by the applicant, such as approaching a women's crisis centre or a family support centre. The applicant could also have brought a claim for compensation against JHL using civil law mechanisms. The state did, however, acknowledge that the investigation of the applicant's complaints had taken too long and that this had resulted in the case ultimately becoming time-barred. It also admitted that 'it was regrettable that the case had not been fully and efficiently investigated and the perpetrator of the alleged crime had not been convicted'.[17] The state therefore presented the ECtHR with a unilateral declaration on 1 September 2011, acknowledging a breach of Article 8. Very interestingly, however, on 5 June 2012, the Court decided not to accept this declaration.

On 26 March 2013, the ECtHR issued its judgment in the case. The first point which the Court addressed was the state's assertion that the applicant's complaints did not fall to be considered under Article 3 due to the 'trivial nature' of the injuries which had been sustained. The ECtHR reiterated that ill-treatment must attain a minimum level of severity in order to fall within the scope of Article 3. However, 'The assessment of this minimum is relative: it depends on all the circumstances of the case, such as the nature and context of the treatment, its duration, its physical and mental effects and, in some instances, the sex, age and state of health of the victim'.[18] The Court proceeded to state that,

16 At para. 55.
17 At para. 61.
18 At para. 65.

> Treatment has been held … to be 'inhuman' because, *inter alia*, it was premeditated, was applied for hours at a stretch and caused either actual bodily injury or intense physical and mental suffering … Treatment has been considered 'degrading' when it was such as to arouse in its victims feelings of fear, anguish and inferiority, capable of humiliating and debasing them and possibly breaking their physical or moral resistance.[19]

Applying these standards to the facts of the case in question, the ECtHR noted the physical violence suffered by the applicant, as a result of which she had sustained hypodermic bruising on the left hip and thigh; a scrape on the right cheek and brachium; bruising on the right eye and cheek, the left temple and the shin; a scrape on the left shin; and hypodermic bruising on her face. The Court also observed that the five incidents of violence had occurred over a one-month time period. In the view of the ECtHR, these incidents therefore constituted a continuing situation, which it regarded as being an aggravating circumstance. The Court also stated that it could not 'turn a blind eye to the psychological aspect of the alleged ill-treatment'.[20] The applicant had made credible assertions that she had been exposed to threats to her physical integrity over a certain period of time and that she had in fact been attacked on five occasions. In this regard, the ECtHR acknowledged that 'psychological impact is an important aspect of … domestic violence'.[21] The Court therefore considered that,

> the ill-treatment of the applicant, which on five occasions caused her physical injuries, combined with her feelings of fear and helplessness, was sufficiently serious to reach the level of severity under Article 3 of the Convention and thus raise the Government's positive obligation under this provision.[22]

The applicant's complaints were thus declared to be admissible under Article 3 of the ECHR. In addition, the ECtHR considered that, as the applicant's complaint under Article 8 was based on the same facts, it must also be declared admissible.

Having found that the level of severity of the ill-treatment suffered by the applicant reached the threshold for the applicability of Article 3, the ECtHR then proceeded to analyse the adequacy of the response by the state. The judgment asserted that,

19 At para. 66.
20 At para. 69.
21 At para. 69.
22 At para. 70.

> Once the Court has found that the level of severity of violence inflicted by private individuals attracts protection under Article 3 of the Convention, its case-law is consistent and clear to the effect that this Article requires the implementation of adequate criminal-law mechanisms.[23]

The ECtHR then reiterated its oft-cited principle that,

> the obligation on the High Contracting Parties under Article 1 of the Convention to secure to everyone within their jurisdiction the rights and freedoms defined in the Convention, taken together with Article 3, requires States to take measures designed to ensure that individuals within their jurisdiction are not subjected to torture or inhuman or degrading treatment or punishment, including such ill-treatment administered by private individuals.[24]

Accordingly, 'Article 3 requires States to put in place effective criminal-law provisions to deter the commission of offences against personal integrity, backed up by law-enforcement machinery for the prevention, suppression and punishment of breaches of such provisions'.[25] The ECtHR went on to assert that, 'In order that a State may be held responsible it must … be shown that the domestic legal system, and in particular the criminal law applicable in the circumstances of the case, failed to provide practical and effective protection of the rights guaranteed by Article 3'.[26]

In applying these principles to the facts of the case in question, the ECtHR professed itself to be satisfied that the national law of Lithuania provided a sufficient regulatory framework to pursue the crimes alleged to have been committed by J.H.L. against the applicant. However, it concluded that the national law had not been implemented in a manner sufficient to protect the applicant's rights. Once the case had been transferred for public prosecution, the investigation had then been suspended twice for lack of evidence. On each occasion, upon the persistent appeals of the applicant, the investigator's decisions had been quashed due to the investigations being insufficiently thorough. The ECtHR found this to be 'a serious flaw on the part of the State'.[27] According to the Court, 'the choice of the means to secure compliance with Article 3 in the sphere of the relations of individuals between themselves is in principle a matter that falls within the domestic authorities' margin of appreciation,

23 At para. 73.
24 At para. 74.
25 At para. 75.
26 At para. 75.
27 At para. 82.

provided that criminal-law mechanisms are available to the victim'.[28] In the ECtHR's view, it was not therefore appropriate for it to speculate on the question of whether the applicant's criminal complaint should have been pursued by the public prosecutor or by way of a private prosecution. Nevertheless, the fact remained that 'the circumstances of the case were never established by a competent court of law'.[29] The ECtHR noted that one of the purposes of imposing criminal sanctions was to deter the offender from causing further harm; however, this aim could not be achieved without having the facts of the case established by a criminal court. The ECtHR thus stated that it could not

> accept that the purpose of effective protection against acts of ill-treatment is achieved where the criminal proceedings are discontinued owing to the fact that the prosecution has become time-barred and where this has occurred … as a result of the flaws in the actions of the relevant State authorities.[30]

It was therefore concluded by the Court that, 'the practices at issue in the present case, together with the manner in which the criminal-law mechanisms were implemented, did not provide adequate protection to the applicant against acts of violence', and that there had thus been a violation of Article 3.[31] The ECtHR stated that, having found a breach of Article 3, it was not necessary to examine the complaint separately under Article 8. The applicant had claimed 20,000 euros in respect of non-pecuniary damage; however, the Court viewed this amount as excessive and instead awarded the applicant 5,000 euros.

The fact that the ECtHR in *Valiuliene* was not content simply to accept the unilateral declaration of the state that there had been a violation of Article 8, but no violation of Article 3 due to what the state termed 'the trivial nature' of the applicant's injuries[32] is praiseworthy. This served to emphasise that the Court viewed domestic abuse as a serious matter and not one to be approached with the lack of gravity with which the state appeared to deal with the matter in the case in question.

However, there were also difficulties with the ECtHR's approach in this case, some of which were highlighted in the Concurring Opinion of Judge Pinto de Albuquerque, who stated that although he voted for the operative part of the judgment, he could not subscribe to its motivation. Essentially, he felt that the case 'raised fundamental legal issues which have not been dealt with

28 At para. 85.
29 At para. 85.
30 At para. 85.
31 At para. 86.
32 At para. 55.

properly by the majority',[33] and that further explanation was needed regarding the application of the ECtHR to cases involving domestic abuse. In a footnote to his Concurring Opinion, Judge Pinto de Albuquerque further stated that,

> The majority missed the opportunity to set out a principled reasoning to impute a violation of Article 3, and not of Article 8, to the respondent State, preferring once again to remain attached to the particular specificities of the case. Yet that reasoning was much needed in view of the current disparate case-law ... Moreover, having rejected the respondent Government's unilateral declaration, which acknowledged a violation of Article 8, the Court had an additional duty to provide a thorough reasoning of its finding of a violation of Article 3.[34]

Essentially one of the main problems with the judgment in *Valiuliene v. Lithuania* is that the Court missed a key opportunity to clarify the rationale behind its use of Articles 3 and 8 in its jurisprudence on domestic abuse. As noted above, until that point the approach of the Court as regards the provisions on which it based its findings of violations of the ECHR in such cases had been somewhat incoherent, particularly in relation to the use of Articles 3 and 8. In certain cases involving domestic abuse, such as *Opuz v. Turkey*[35] and *E.S. and Others v. Slovakia*,[36] the ECtHR had found breaches of Article 3. Nevertheless, equally there were other cases, such as *Bevacqua and S v. Bulgaria*, *A v. Croatia,* and *Kalucza v. Hungary*, in which the Court had found violations of Article 8 only and also refrained from examining the cases under Article 3. In *Valiuliene v. Lithuania* however, the ECtHR did exactly the opposite and stated that it was not necessary to examine the complaint under Article 8, as it had already found a violation of Article 3. The difficulty is that the Court's reasoning for this difference in approach was not explained in its judgment.

On the facts of *Valiuliene v. Lithuania*, there appeared to be nothing to distinguish the abuse suffered by the applicant from that which had been experienced by the applicants in other cases involving domestic abuse in which arguments had been made in respect of *inter alia* Articles 3 and 8, and in which the ECtHR had based its findings on breaches of Article 8 only. For example, in *Bevacqua and S v. Bulgaria* the application had been submitted by the first applicant on her own behalf and also on behalf of her son S. The first applicant had married her husband, referred to in the judgment as Mr N, in 1995 and given birth to S in January 1997. However, Mr N had

33 Concurring Opinion of Judge Pinto de Albuquerque.

34 Concurring Opinion of Judge Pinto de Albuquerque, at footnote 18.

35 The Court also found violations of Articles 2 and 14 in this case.

36 The Court also found a violation of Article 8 in this case.

become aggressive, and on 1 March 2000, the first applicant had left the family home with her son and moved into her parents' apartment. Nevertheless, more instances of violence followed, and the injuries sustained by the first applicant had included bruising of her eyelid, face, arm and hip and swelling of her cheek. It had been alleged that the authorities had failed to protect the first applicant from the violent behaviour of her former husband and had failed to take the necessary measures to secure respect for the family life of both applicants. It had therefore been argued that the state had violated *inter alia* Articles 3 and 8 of the ECHR.

The ECtHR examined the complaints under Article 8, but not under Article 3. In holding that there had been a violation of Article 8, the Court stated that,

> At the relevant time Bulgarian law did not provide for specific administrative and policing measures (in relation to domestic abuse) and the measures taken by the police and prosecuting authorities on the basis of their general powers did not prove effective … In the Court's view, the authorities' failure to impose sanctions or otherwise enforce Mr N.'s obligation to refrain from unlawful acts was critical in the circumstances of this case, as it amounted to a refusal to provide the immediate assistance the applicants needed. The authorities' view that no such assistance was due as the dispute concerned a 'private matter' was incompatible with their positive obligations to secure the enjoyment of the applicants' Article 8 rights.[37]

Four thousand euros were awarded in respect of non-pecuniary damage and 3,000 euros in respect of costs and expenses. In this case, the severity of the applicant's injuries seemed to be fairly similar to that of the injuries of the applicant in *Valiuliene v. Lithuania*, and the attacks were carried out over a longer period of time than in the *Valiuliene* case.

Likewise, in *A v. Croatia*, the ECtHR had held that having found a violation of Article 8, there was no need to consider the case under Articles 2, 3 or 13, in respect of which the applicant had also alleged violations. In this case, the applicant had complained that the authorities had failed to protect her against the domestic abuse of her ex-husband despite being aware of his repeated physical and verbal assaults and death threats. The applicant's ex-husband had suffered from severe mental disorders and, between November 2003 and June 2006, he had subjected the applicant to repeated violent behaviour. The abuse was both physical, including kicking and hitting the applicant in the head, face and body; and also verbal, including making serious death threats against the applicant. Various proceedings were brought against the applicant's ex-husband in the national courts, and measures such as restraining

37 (App. No. 71127/01), judgment of 12 September 2008, at para. 83.

orders, psychiatric or psychosocial treatment and a prison term were ordered. However, only some of these orders had actually been implemented. The applicant alleged that the authorities had failed to protect her adequately from domestic abuse and argued that the state was thereby in violation of Articles 2, 3, 8, 13 and 14 of the ECHR.

The ECtHR held that the authorities' failure to implement the measures ordered by the national courts, aimed both at addressing the psychiatric condition of the applicant's ex-husband and also at providing the applicant with protection against further violence, had left her for a prolonged period in a situation in which her right to respect for her private life under Article 8 had been violated. However, having found a breach of Article 8, the Court stated that it was not necessary to examine the complaint under Articles 2, 3 or 13. The ECtHR did, however, declare that the applicant's complaint of a violation of Article 14 was inadmissible, as she had not provided sufficient evidence, such as reports or statistics, to establish that the measures and practices adopted by the state against domestic abuse, or the effects of such measures or practices, were discriminatory. The applicant was awarded 9,000 euros in respect of non-pecuniary damage and 4,470 euros in respect of costs and expenses. Again, the violent attacks against the applicant in this case had been carried out over a much longer period of time than were the attacks against the applicant in *Valiuliene*. Also, it seems that the injuries in question in *A v. Croatia* had been of a more severe nature. Why then was a violation of solely Article 8 found in *A v. Croatia*, while the Court was so adamant that it was necessary to find a breach of Article 3 in *Valiuliene*?

The ECtHR had adopted the same approach as in *A v. Croatia* in *Kalucza v. Hungary*, another case involving domestic abuse in which the applicant had argued that the state was in violation of Articles 2, 3, 8 and 13 of the ECHR. Again, the Court found a breach of Article 8 and then proceeded to state that as a consequence it was unnecessary to examine the case under Articles 2, 3 or 13. At the time of the ECtHR's judgment in this case, the applicant had unwillingly been sharing a flat with her violent ex-partner, referred to in the judgment as GyB, pending the outcome of numerous civil disputes concerning the ownership of the flat. Following her divorce, the applicant had begun a relationship with GyB in April 2005. At that time, she had shared joint ownership of the flat with her ex-husband; however, at the start of the relationship between the applicant and GyB, the latter had decided to pay the ex-husband's share in the flat. GyB had officially acquired ownership of this share in January 2006 and the flat had been registered as his place of residence in November 2006. The relationship between the applicant and GyB had ended around January 2007. Since then, GyB had continued to stay in the flat against the applicant's wishes. The applicant had requested the help of the relevant authorities on numerous occasions and had lodged criminal complaints against GyB for rape, assault and harassment. On two occasions, GyB had been found guilty of assault, released on parole and ordered to pay a fine. On three occasions, the applicant herself had been found guilty of disorderly conduct, assault and causing grievous bodily harm. The applicant had made two requests for a restraining order to be issued against GyB. Her first request, which had been made in June 2008, had been dismissed by the courts in January 2010 on the ground that both parties were responsible for their bad relationship. Her second request had also been dismissed for the same reason. Between October 2005 and August 2010, 13 medical reports had been drawn up which recorded contusions mostly to the applicant's head, face, chest and neck. The applicant had argued that the state was in violation of Articles 2, 3, 8 and 13, due to the failure of the authorities to protect her from constant physical and psychological abuse in her home.

In its judgment, the ECtHR noted that it had taken the Hungarian authorities more than one and a half years to decide on the applicant's first request for a restraining order, despite the fact that the fundamental reason behind such a measure was to provide prompt protection to victims of violence. In addition, insufficient reasons had been given for the dismissal of the requests, the courts merely relying on the fact that both parties had been involved in assaults against each other. As the ECtHR pointed out, if such an order could not have been made in the event of a mutual assault, the possibility of the victim having acted in legitimate self-defence would have been ruled out, thus seriously undermining the aim of providing effective protection to victims. The national courts had also failed to comply with their obligation to decide on the civil cases concerning the flat within a reasonable time. Even though the applicant had lodged criminal complaints against her partner for assault, had repeatedly requested that restraining orders be brought against him and had brought civil proceedings to order his eviction from the flat, the authorities had failed to adopt sufficient measures to secure the effective protection of the applicant. There had thus been a violation of Article 8. Having thereby found a breach of Article 8, the ECtHR stated that it was therefore also unnecessary to examine the applicant's complaint under Articles 2, 3 or 13. The Court proceeded to award the applicant the sum of 5,150 euros in respect of non-pecuniary damage with regard to the violation of Article 8. Again, the violence in question in this case had been carried out over a much longer period of time than the abuse against the applicant in *Valiuliene,* and the injuries suffered by the applicant in *Kalucza* appeared, if anything, to have been more severe than those sustained by the applicant in *Valiuliene.*

The question arises, therefore, why the ECtHR adopted such an approach in *Bevacqua and S v. Bulgaria*, *A v. Croatia,* and *Kalucza v. Hungary*. As noted above, it is likely that the reason was based purely on practicality, in that it can be somewhat easier to establish a breach of Article 8 than it is to establish a violation of Article 3. However, the difficulty was that an approach based on expediency could be misinterpreted as being based on principle, with that principle being that domestic abuse is only serious enough to be conceptualised as a breach of Article 8, but does not in the majority of cases meet the threshold of constituting a violation of Article 3. This was problematic, to say the least. Indeed, there was evidence in the case of *Valiuliene v. Lithuania* itself that the practice of the ECtHR was being interpreted in this manner. In her dissenting opinion in the case, Judge Jociene stated that she was of the view that 'the Court has incorrectly relied on Article 3 in the circumstances of the present case' and that, 'This position of the Chamber is not supported by the Court's case-law, where domestic violence cases are mostly examined from the perspective of Article 8 of the Convention'.[38] Judge Jociene went on to say that,

> Accordingly, and referring to the Court's case-law on the subject … the applicant's complaint in connection with the physical attacks on her should have been examined under Article 8 of the Convention and the applicant's right to respect for her private life.[39]

It is clear therefore that Judge Jociene was of the view that the general practice of the ECtHR was to use Article 8 in cases of domestic abuse, as opposed to Article 3, and that this approach was grounded on principle as opposed to being based purely on practical considerations. Equally, in accepting that there had been a breach of Article 8 in the case but not a violation of Article 3, it is not inconceivable that the state may have consulted the Court's previous case law on domestic abuse and concluded that it was probable that a violation of Article 8 would be found, and that the case would not be analysed under Article 3. The fact that the state seemed to be of the view that abuse constituting a violation of Article 8 could still be described as resulting in injuries that are 'merely trivial' in nature was troubling, and raised concerns over the message which the Court's use of Article 8 in cases of domestic abuse had sent out to states.

Whatever the reason for the Court's approach in its previous case law involving domestic abuse, the question arises of why a different approach was adopted in *Valiuliene v. Lithuania*. In this instance, the ECtHR again limited its consideration to one article of the ECHR; however, this time it chose Article 3 as opposed to Article 8 as the provision to be applied. However, why was the ECtHR so adamant that a violation of Article 3 had been established in this particular instance? As discussed above, on the facts of the case, there appeared to be nothing to distinguish the abuse suffered by the applicant from that experienced by the applicants in other cases involving domestic abuse in which the Court had based its judgments on Article 8, in terms of the intensity of the abuse or the severity of the injuries sustained. Indeed, the ECtHR itself does not seem to have viewed the abuse sustained by the

38 Dissenting Opinion of Judge Jociene, at para. 10.
39 Dissenting Opinion of Judge Jociene, at para. 11.

applicant in *Valiuliene* as more severe than that suffered by the applicants in the cases involving domestic abuse discussed above, as seen in the levels of compensation for non-pecuniary damage awarded by the Court in these cases. In *Valiuliene,* the ECtHR awarded the applicant 5,000 euros for non-pecuniary damage in respect of the breach of Article 3. In *Bevacqua and S v. Bulgaria, A v. Croatia,* and *Kalucza v. Hungary*, the applicants had been awarded 4,000, 9,000 and 5,150 euros respectively for non-pecuniary damage regarding the violations of Article 8. The level of non-pecuniary damage awarded in *Valiuliene* was therefore lower than that which was awarded in *Kalucza* and significantly lower than that which was awarded in *A v. Croatia.*

It seems that the most likely explanation for the Court's change in approach regarding *Valiuliene v. Lithuania* lies with the actions of the state in submitting the unilateral declaration accepting that there had been a violation of Article 8 but stating that there had been no breach of Article 3. It must be remembered that in the cases involving domestic abuse in which the ECtHR had found a violation of Article 8 and then omitted to examine Article 3, it was by no means saying that a breach of Article 3 could not be substantiated. It was merely stating that having found a violation of the ECHR with respect of one article, it was unnecessary to examine the case under any other provisions. If, however, the Court had simply accepted the state's unilateral declaration of a breach of Article 8 in *Valiuliene v. Lithuania* without further examination, it would, implicitly at least, be accepting that there had been no violation of Article 3 in this instance. It seems that such an outcome was not desired by the ECtHR. Indeed, not only did the Court refuse to accept the state's unilateral declaration, but it also proceeded to make findings in its judgment that were, in a sense, the polar opposite of what the state had asserted in its unilateral declaration. Instead of agreeing that there had been a violation of Article 8, but not of Article 3, the Court held that there had been a breach of Article 3 and that it was not therefore necessary to examine whether there had also been a violation of Article 8.

It appears likely that the Court's approach in *Valiuliene v. Lithuania* was influenced to a large extent by the attitude which the state seemed to exhibit in making its unilateral declaration. In making the declaration, the state claimed that although it accepted that there had been a violation of Article 8, there had been no violation of Article 3 due to what it termed 'the trivial nature' of the applicant's injuries.[40] It appeared that the state was therefore minimising the seriousness of what was, even on its own admission, a human rights violation. As the ECtHR itself pointed out, in assessing the minimum level of severity of abuse needed to fall within the scope of Article 3, all the circumstances of the case must be taken into consideration, including 'the nature and context of the

40 At para. 55.

treatment, its duration, its physical and mental effects and, in some instances, the sex, age and state of health of the victim'.[41] In claiming that there had been no violation of Article 3, the state had failed to take into account the circumstances which surround situations involving domestic abuse, in particular, the psychological impact which such abuse has on the victim. The ECtHR may well have wished to distance itself from the views of the state in this regard, and the most effective way of doing so was arguably to find a violation of Article 3 only and hold that it was therefore unnecessary to examine the applicability of Article 8.

It is interesting to speculate on the question of what approach the ECtHR would have adopted in this case had the state not submitted its unilateral declaration. It is, of course, impossible to know how the Court would have responded in the absence of such a declaration, and so this question can only ever be a matter of conjecture. Nevertheless, given the ECtHR's history in dealing with cases involving domestic abuse, it is not inconceivable that the ECtHR would have adopted a similar approach to its judgments in *Bevacqua and S v. Bulgaria*, *A v. Croatia* and *Kalucza v. Hungary*, in which the Court had found violations of Article 8 and then stated that it was not necessary to also examine the cases under Article 3. If the ECtHR had adopted such an approach in *Valiuliene v. Lithuania*, it is unlikely that it would have done so with the intention of implying that the abuse in question was insufficient to amount to a violation of Article 3, or that the situation was less serious than a finding of a breach of Article 3 would have inferred. Nevertheless, in making its unilateral declaration, the state seemed to be of the view that being found in violation of Article 8 would be a less serious matter than being found to be in breach of Article 3. The state may, therefore, have 'shot itself in the foot', so to speak, by making its unilateral declaration in this case. In doing so, it is possible that the state actually spurred the ECtHR into finding a violation of Article 3 in order to emphasise the seriousness of domestic abuse.

As discussed above and as pointed out by Judge Pinto de Albuquerque in his concurring opinion, one of the difficulties with the Court's judgment in *Valiuliene v. Lithuania* is that the ECtHR failed to set out a principled rationale for its use of the various ECHR provisions, particularly Articles 3 and 8, as bases for finding violations in cases involving domestic abuse. However, it is likely that one of the main reasons for the ECtHR's omission in this respect is that, in reality, it is impossible to rationalise the somewhat haphazard case law in any kind of reasoned manner. As discussed above, there seems to be no explanation in principle as to why Article 8 violations were found in *Bevacqua and S v. Bulgaria, A v. Croatia* and *Kalucza v. Hungary*, while the finding of a breach of Article 8 was insufficient in *Valiuliene v. Lithuania*, as demonstrated by the Court's refusal to accept the state's unilateral declaration

41 At para. 65.

in this regard. Indeed, it seems likely that the reasoning behind the findings of violations of Article 8 only was purely a matter of expediency. In the absence of a principled rationale for its approach, there is in reality no explanation that could be given by the ECtHR. Nevertheless, this should not detract from the merits of the Court's resolute attitude in *Valiuliene v. Lithuania*. It is much to the ECtHR's credit that it did not accept the state's unilateral declaration and instead chose to examine the case under Article 3 only, even though such a course of action constituted a departure from its previous jurisprudence.

It could perhaps be argued that to an individual applicant, the crucial issue of concern is whether the ECtHR finds a violation of the ECHR, and the question of whether the violation is of Article 3 or of Article 8 is of no great significance. This argument is indeed valid to a certain extent. If the Court finds a violation of any provision of the ECHR and awards compensation to the applicant, it is likely that the applicant will feel vindicated, at least to some degree. In a footnote to his concurring opinion in *Valiuliene v. Lithuania*, Judge Pinto de Albuquerque commented that the issue of which articles the ECtHR bases its findings on is 'obviously not irrelevant, for compensation and other purposes'.[42] However, as discussed above, it seems that, at least in domestic abuse cases, the question of which provision the Court grounds its finding of a violation on makes no difference to the amount of compensation awarded to the individual applicant. Nevertheless, the significance of this issue stretches beyond the issue of compensation. It is arguable that a finding on the part of the ECtHR that domestic abuse constitutes a violation of the non-derogable right to be free from torture or inhuman or degrading treatment or punishment sends out a stronger message to states regarding the seriousness with which the Court regards this issue than does a finding that domestic abuse breaches the right to respect for private and family life. Indeed, in rejecting the state's unilateral declaration of a violation of Article 8 in *Valiuliene*, the ECtHR seemed to realise this to be the case.

Since the judgment of the ECtHR in *Valiuliene*, the Court has certainly made considerably more use of Article 3 in cases involving domestic abuse. Interestingly, seven months after its judgment in *Valiuliene*, the ECtHR issued its judgment in another case against Lithuania, *D.P. v. Lithuania*,[43] in which the state again admitted that it was in violation of the ECHR due to a failure to respond adequately to a situation involving domestic abuse. Again it submitted a unilateral declaration; however, this time the declaration acknowledged that the breach was of Article 3. The ECtHR accepted the declaration and struck out the application. Following the judgment in *Valiuliene*, within a short space of time violations of Article 3 were also found in five domestic

42 Concurring Opinion of Judge Pinto de Albuquerque, at footnote 18.
43 (App. No. 27920/08), judgment of 22 October 2013.

abuse cases against Moldova, the judgments in which were issued between July 2013 and January 2014.[44]

Conceptualising Domestic Abuse as Torture

However, it is argued that although conceptualisations of domestic abuse in the case law of the ECtHR have evolved greatly in a very meritorious manner, further development of the Court's conceptualisation of this issue is still needed. Despite the fact that it has now been firmly established that domestic abuse falls within the scope of Article 3, the Court has not yet expressly found in any case involving domestic abuse that such abuse violates the 'torture' limb of this provision, as distinct from 'inhuman or degrading treatment'. In *Volodina v. Russia*[45] and *Tunikova and Others v. Russia*,[46] both of which involved domestic abuse, questions arose as to whether the ECtHR should have expressly found violations of the 'torture' limb of Article 3.

The ECtHR issued its judgment in *Volodina v. Russia*[47] in July 2019. The applicant in this case had, in November 2014, commenced a relationship with a man referred to in the judgment as S, and they began living together in Ulyanovsk. In May 2015, the applicant moved out, whereupon S threatened to kill both the applicant and her son if she refused to return to live with him. In January 2016, the applicant complained to the police that S had broken the windscreen of her car; however, the police did not institute criminal proceedings as S replaced the damaged windscreen. The applicant then moved to Moscow. She published her curriculum vitae on a number of job-hunting websites, and a person referred to in the judgment as D invited her to what she believed was a job interview. D collected the applicant in his car; however, S then appeared from the back of the car and brought the applicant back to Ulyanovsk after taking her mobile phone and personal effects. Following their return to Ulyanovsk, S punched the applicant in the stomach and face. She was taken to hospital and it was established that she was nine weeks pregnant, but that there was a risk of miscarriage. The applicant underwent an abortion.

44 *Eremia and Others v. Moldova* (App. No. 3564/11), judgment of 28 May 2013; *B. v. Moldova* (App. No. 61382/09), judgment of 16 July 2013; *Mudric v. Moldova* (App. No. 74839/10), judgment of 16 July 2013; *N.A. v. Moldova* (App. No. 13424/06), judgment of 24 September 2013; and *T.M. and C.M. v. Moldova* (App. No. 26608/11), judgment of 28 January 2014.

45 (App. No. 41261/17), judgment of 9 July 2019.

46 (App. Nos. 55974/16, 53118/17, 27484/18, 28011/19), judgment of 14 December 2021.

47 (App. No. 41261/17), judgment of 9 July 2019. For a discussion of this case, see also McQuigg R., 'The European Court of Human Rights and Domestic Violence: *Volodina v. Russia*' (2021) 10 *International Human Rights Law Review* 155; and McQuigg R, 'The Evolving Jurisprudence of the European Court of Human Rights on Domestic Abuse' in Czech P., Herschl L., Lukas K., Nowak,M. and Oberleitner G. (eds), *European Yearbook on Human Rights*, 2022, Intersentia, Cambridge, 205 at 209–213.

She reported the violence to the police; however, she later withdrew her complaints and no further action was taken.

In May 2016, S punched the applicant in the stomach, pushed her to the ground and began to choke her. The applicant complained to the police; however, no criminal proceedings were instigated, as the police were of the view that no prosecutable offence had been committed. Later that month, the applicant returned to Moscow in an attempt to hide from S; however, in July 2016 he found and attacked her. Neighbours who had witnessed the attack called the police, and the applicant lodged a criminal complaint against S, reporting that he had been violent and had threatened to kill her. In August 2016, S sent a text message to the applicant, stating that he had damaged the braking system of her car. The applicant called the police, and an officer arrived and took stock of the extent of the damage. However, again the police declined to prosecute S.

In September 2016, the applicant discovered an electronic device in the lining of her bag, which she believed was a GPS tracking device placed there by S. She reported her concerns to an Investigative Committee in Moscow, which forwarded the report to the police; however, no inquiry was initiated. In early 2018, S placed the applicant's private photographs on a social network without her consent, and in March 2018, the police initiated a criminal investigation for invasion of personal privacy.

On 12 March 2018, the applicant reported to the police that she had received threatening calls from S the previous night and that he had been in front of her home earlier that day. On 21 March, the police declined to commence a criminal investigation as they believed that there had been no danger of S carrying out the threat to kill the applicant, due to the fact that she had remained in her flat and S had stayed in his car. Also on 21 March, the applicant called a taxi in order to visit a friend. S followed the taxi, pulled the applicant out, and began dragging her towards his car. The applicant sprayed tear gas in his face, whereupon he pushed her several times, took her bag, and drove off with it. The applicant lodged a complaint with the police concerning the attack and the theft of her bag, which had contained identity documents and two mobile phones. S then arrived at the police station and returned the bag to the applicant. The next day he brought the phones to the police, who returned them to the applicant, and the latter found her identity documents in her mailbox. In April 2018, the police decided not to open an investigation into the alleged theft as the property had been returned. It was also decided that proceedings should not be instigated concerning the threats, on the basis that neither the statements made by S nor his actions constituted sufficient evidence that the death threats had been real. In August 2018, the applicant legally changed her name in order to prevent S from being able to locate her.

Under Chapter 16 of the Russian Criminal Code, there were three levels of assault occasioning actual bodily harm. 'Grievous bodily harm', as found in Article 111, could involve the loss of a body part or the termination of pregnancy; 'medium bodily harm', as found in Article 112, was bodily harm leading to a long-term health disorder or loss of the ability to work; while 'minor bodily harm', as found in Article 115, encompassed injuries taking up to three weeks to heal. Although causing grievous or medium bodily harm was subject to public prosecution, the offence of 'minor bodily harm' was liable only to private prosecution. This meant that it was up to the victim to identify the perpetrator, collect the necessary evidence, secure testimony from witnesses and bring charges before a court. Assault which caused physical pain without resulting in actual bodily harm was regarded as 'battery' under Article 116. Aggravated battery encompassed battery committed for racial, ethnic, social or disorderly motives, and was a criminal offence. However non-aggravated battery was not criminalised and was an administrative offence only.

The applicant argued before the ECtHR that the Russian authorities had failed to protect her from repeated acts of domestic abuse and to hold the perpetrator accountable. She asserted that the Russian authorities had failed to establish a legislative framework to address domestic abuse and had also failed to investigate and prosecute her ill-treatment under the existing criminal-law provisions. In its judgment, the Court stated that the treatment in question reached a level so as to come within the ambit of Article 3, and proceeded to consider whether the state had fulfilled its obligations to protect the applicant from such treatment. The ECtHR was of the view that,

> the Russian legal framework – which does not define domestic violence whether as a separate offence or an aggravating element of other offences and establishes a minimum threshold of gravity of injuries required for launching public prosecution – falls short of the requirements inherent in the State's positive obligation to establish and apply effectively a system punishing all forms of domestic violence and providing sufficient safeguards for victims.[48]

The Court emphasised that requiring injuries to be of a certain level of severity before a criminal investigation can be initiated provides inadequate protection to victims, as some forms of domestic abuse, such as psychological and financial abuse, do not involve physical injury. The ECtHR also stated that,

> A private prosecution puts an excessive burden on the victim of domestic violence, shifting onto her the responsibility for collecting evidence capable of establishing the abuser's guilt to the criminal standard of proof … the challenge becomes unsurmountable for a victim who is expected to

48 At para. 85.

> collect evidence on her own while continuing to live under the same roof as the perpetrator, being financially dependent on him, and fearing reprisals on his part.[49]

The Court then considered whether the state had fulfilled its duty to adopt 'the reasonable measures that might have been expected in order to avert a real and immediate risk of ill-treatment of which the authorities knew or ought to have known'.[50] The ECtHR was of the view that due to the repeated complaints which the applicant had made to the police, the authorities ought to have been aware of the violence to which the applicant had been subjected and of the real and immediate risk that such abuse could recur. The question therefore arose of whether the state had adopted reasonable measures to protect the applicant. The ECtHR pointed out that measures such as restraining orders or protection orders were not available in Russian law. The Court stated that the response of the authorities had been 'manifestly inadequate'[51] and that the state had failed in its duty to investigate the ill-treatment which the applicant had suffered. The ECtHR therefore concluded that there had been a violation of Article 3.[52]

Volodina v. Russia constituted a valuable addition to the jurisprudence of the ECtHR on domestic abuse. It was a strong judgment that reinforced the positive obligations which states have to protect victims of this form of abuse. However, *Volodina* again raises questions regarding how domestic abuse is conceptualised by the ECtHR. In a separate opinion issued by Judge Pinto de Albuquerque, the Judge expressed his view that, although a violation of Article 3 was found in the case, it should have been held that the ill-treatment suffered by the applicant went beyond inhuman or degrading treatment and reached the threshold for torture. In *Ireland v. United Kingdom*, the Court stated that torture consists of 'deliberate inhuman treatment causing very serious and cruel suffering'.[53] In the view of Judge Pinto de Albuquerque, this threshold was met in the instant case. As the Judge stated, the applicant,

> was subjected to multiple and persistent instances of extreme domestic violence, including a punch to her stomach, which in fact led to medical advice that she should induce the abortion of her unborn baby. She was further psychologically taunted through the publication of private photographs, the finding of what was believed to be a GPS tracker inside her

49 At para. 82.
50 At para. 77.
51 At para. 91.
52 A violation of Article 14, taken in conjunction with Article 3, was also found, as is discussed in Chapter 3.
53 (App. No. 5310/71), judgment of 18 January 1978, at para. 167.

purse, threats to kill her – which S. attempted to substantiate by damaging her car – and abduction from her city of residence.[54]

In support of his view, Judge Pinto de Albuquerque cited General Comment 2 of the UN Committee against Torture, which asserts that a state's systematic acquiescence to privately inflicted harm raises concerns under the UN Convention against Torture and other Cruel, Inhuman or Degrading Treatment or Punishment.[55] Indeed the Committee against Torture included violence against women as a principal area of concern in its Concluding Observations on the sixth periodic report submitted by the Russian Federation. The Committee expressed its concern at 'the absence of a definition of domestic violence in the State party's legislation' and at 'reports that police officers are often unwilling to register complaints of domestic violence and even discourage victims from submitting them, and that victims continue to be compelled to participate in reconciliation processes with the perpetrators'.[56]

It does seem that the argument of Judge Pinto de Albuquerque has much to commend it. As the Judge asserted, 'When severe forms of pain and suffering are deliberately inflicted on a person, this must be identified as torture'.[57] In the majority judgment in *Volodina*, the ECtHR referred to the need to adopt a 'gender-sensitive approach' when applying the ECHR to cases involving issues such as domestic abuse.[58] It is certainly arguable that the adoption of such an approach should involve the recognition of 'the gravity and effect of persisting patterns of domestic violence'.[59] As Judge Pinto de Albuquerque commented, 'If the State faces condemnation for allowing its women to be submitted to torture, the positive obligation to protect is even more stringent'.[60]

The question of whether domestic abuse should be specifically conceptualised as torture arose again in the judgment of the ECtHR in *Tunikova and Others v. Russia* in December 2021.[61] In this case the applicants had sustained bodily injuries, including one case of severe mutilation, at the hands of their former partners or husbands, as well as receiving death threats from them. In holding that there had been a breach of Article 3, the ECtHR found that

54 Separate Opinion of Judge Pinto de Albuquerque, joined by Judge Dedov, at para. 7.

55 Committee against Torture, General Comment No. 2, 24 January 2008, CAT/C/GC/2, at para. 18.

56 Committee against Torture, Concluding observations on the sixth periodic report of the Russian Federation, 28 August 2018, CAT/C/RUS/CO/6, at para. 30.

57 Separate Opinion of Judge Pinto de Albuquerque, joined by Judge Dedov, at para. 8.

58 At para 111.

59 At para. 8 of the Separate Opinion of Judge Pinto de Albuquerque, joined by Judge Dedov.

60 At para. 9 of the Separate Opinion of Judge Pinto de Albuquerque, joined by Judge Dedov.

61 (App. Nos. 55974/16, 53118/17, 27484/18, 28011/19), judgment of 14 December 2021.

lised by the Court as torture. The stance of the ECtHR on domestic abuse has certainly evolved greatly.

the state had failed to establish a legal framework to combat domestic abuse effectively; had not assessed the risks of recurrent violence; and had not carried out an effective investigation into the domestic abuse.[62]

Three of the four applicants argued that they had been subjected to 'particularly extreme forms of domestic abuse which caused them very serious and cruel suffering' and which amounted to 'torture' as opposed to 'inhuman or degrading treatment'.[63] In their view, 'recognising severe instances of domestic violence as "torture" would emphasise the gravity of the abuse in the eyes of the public and the authorities tasked with monitoring and response, empower victims, and discourage or even deter perpetrators'.[64] In response, however, the ECtHR stated that,

> the additional characterisation, although important for the applicants and capable of influencing the public perception of domestic violence, is not necessary in the circumstances of the present case, in which there is no doubt that the treatment inflicted on the applicants attained the necessary threshold of severity to fall within the scope of Article 3 of the Convention.[65]

Nevertheless, the issue that arose in *Volodina* and *Tunikova* regarding whether domestic abuse should be specifically conceptualised as torture, as opposed to inhuman or degrading treatment, is also illustrative of the evolution of the case law of the ECtHR. It is now beyond doubt that cases of domestic abuse will usually fall within the scope of Article 3; rather, the question has become whether domestic abuse should be expressly held to come within the 'torture' limb of this provision. It is certainly arguable that this would be a very welcome development, as it would make a strong statement concerning the seriousness of this issue. Indeed, a number of commentators have likened domestic abuse to torture.[66] It is notable that in certain cases, such as *Ireland v. United Kingdom*,[67] a state has attempted (albeit unsuccessfully) to admit to inhuman or degrading treatment in the hope that the ECtHR would not then consider whether the ill-treatment in question actually reached the threshold

62 A violation of Article 14, taken in conjunction with Article 3, was also found.

63 At para. 71.

64 At para. 71.

65 At para. 77.

66 See, for example, Copelon R., 'Intimate Terror: Understanding Domestic Violence as Torture', in Cook R. (ed.), *Human Rights of Women – National and International Perspectives,* 1994, University of Pennsylvania Press, Philadelphia, 116; and Grdinic E., 'Application of the Elements of Torture and Other Forms of Ill-Treatment, as Defined by the European Court and Commission of Human Rights, to the Incidents of Domestic Violence' (2000) 23 *Hastings International and Comparative Law Review* 217.

67 (App. No. 5310/71), judgment of 18 January 1978.

of constituting torture. It is possible that a state could attempt to make such an argument in a case involving domestic abuse, thus prompting the ECtHR to make a definitive ruling on this issue, much in the same way that the state's unilateral declaration in *Valiuliene* prompted a change in the Court's approach regarding the use of Article 3 in domestic abuse cases.

Conceptualising Domestic Abuse as Coercive Control

As was discussed in Chapter 1, it has now been recognised by many scholars and groups seeking to support victims of domestic abuse that such abuse encompasses not only physical violence but should instead be conceptualised as involving broader patterns of coercive and controlling behaviour.[68] As Fitz-Gibbon, Walklate and McCulloch comment, 'Coercive control illuminates domestic abuse as a pattern of behaviours, within which physical violence may exist alongside a range of other abusive behaviours'.[69] The tactics of perpetrators of coercive control may include emotional abuse, such as blaming the victim or undermining her self-esteem; verbal abuse; economic abuse, for example, controlling all finances; and physical violence.[70] As Herring states, 'Fear is often at the heart of coercive control and is its primary vehicle. Violence may or may not, be used as one tool'.[71] Due to such considerations, a number of jurisdictions have enacted legislation criminalising coercive and controlling behaviour.[72]

It is notable that a recognition of domestic abuse as coercive control can also be seen in statements made by UN bodies. Indeed, as far back as 1992, prior to more widespread recognition of the concept of coercive control, the CEDAW Committee demonstrated an understanding in its General

68 For a discussion of the concept of coercive control, see Stark E., *Coercive Control: How Men Trap Women in Personal Life*, 2007, Oxford University Press, Oxford; Stark E., 'Rethinking Coercive Control' (2009) 15 *Violence Against Women* 1509; Williamson E., 'Living in the World of the Domestic Violence Perpetrator: Negotiating the Unreality of Coercive Control' (2010) 16 *Violence Against Women* 1412; Stark E., 'Looking Beyond Domestic Violence: Policing Coercive Control' (2012) 12 *Journal of Police Crisis Negotiations* 199; and Stark E. and Hester M., 'Coercive Control: Update and Review' (2019) 25 *Violence Against Women* 81.

69 Fitz-Gibbon K., Walklate S. and McCulloch J., 'Editorial Introduction', (2018) 18 *Criminology and Criminal Justice* 3 at 3.

70 Jeffries S., 'In the Best Interests of the Abuser: Coercive Control, Child Custody Proceedings and the "Expert" Assessments that Guide Judicial Determinations' (2016) 5 *Laws* 14 at 15.

71 Herring, op. cit., at 27.

72 Coercive and controlling behaviour was criminalised in England and Wales under section 76 of the Serious Crime Act 2015; abusive behaviour (including psychological abuse) towards a partner or ex-partner was criminalised in Scotland under section 1 of the Domestic Abuse (Scotland) Act 2018; and a domestic abuse offence which essentially criminalised coercive and controlling behaviour was enacted in Northern Ireland under section 1 of the Domestic Abuse and Civil Proceedings Act (Northern Ireland) 2021.

Recommendation No. 19 that gender-based violence includes 'acts that inflict … mental … harm or suffering' and 'coercion'.[73] Similarly, in its General Recommendation No. 35 on gender-based violence against women, which was issued in 2017, the CEDAW Committee asserted that gender-based violence 'takes multiple forms, including acts or omissions intended or likely to cause or result in … psychological or economic harm or suffering to women' and 'coercion'.[74] Indeed, General Recommendation No. 35 recommended that states parties to CEDAW, 'Ensure that all forms of gender-based violence against women in all spheres, which amount to a violation of their … psychological integrity, are criminalized and introduce, without delay, or strengthen legal sanctions commensurate with the gravity of the offence as well as civil remedies'.[75] Two years later, in its 2019 Concluding Observations on the UK's eighth periodic report, the CEDAW Committee expressed concern in relation to the legislative position regarding gender-based violence in Northern Ireland, in which coercive control had not been criminalised at the time, and recommended that the UK, 'Adopt legislative and comprehensive policy measures to protect women from all forms of gender-based violence throughout the State party's jurisdiction, including Northern Ireland'.[76]

Similarly, in the influential UN Declaration on the Elimination of Violence against Women, which was issued by the UN General Assembly in 1993, it was recognised that the definition of 'violence against women' should not be limited to physical violence, but should encompass 'coercion' and acts that result in, or are likely to result in, 'psychological harm or suffering to women'.[77] In this Declaration, 'violence against women' included various forms of domestic abuse, including 'psychological violence'.[78] In addition, the Platform for Action, which resulted from the Fourth World Conference on Women held in 1995 in Beijing, urged states to adopt a wide range of measures regarding violence against women, with this term again being defined as including 'coercion' and gender-based violence resulting in, or likely to result in, 'psychological harm or suffering to women'.[79]

73 UN Committee on the Elimination of Discrimination Against Women, 'General Recommendation No. 19: Violence against women' (1992), para. 6. General Recommendation No. 19 was discussed further in Chapter 1.

74 UN Committee on the Elimination of Discrimination Against Women, 'General recommendation No. 35 on gender-based violence against women, updating general recommendation No. 19' (2017), para. 14.

75 Para. 29.

76 Committee on the Elimination of Discrimination Against Women, 'Concluding observations on the eighth periodic report of the United Kingdom of Great Britain and Northern Ireland', CEDAW/C/GBR/CO/8 (14 March 2019), para. 30(b).

77 Declaration on the Elimination of Violence against Women, General Assembly Resolution 48/104 (20 December 1993), Article 1.

78 Article 2.

79 Beijing Platform for Action, U.N. Doc.A/CONF.177/20 (1995), para. 113.

In the context of the Council of Europe, Article 33 of the Istanbul Convention places an obligation on state parties to criminalise coercive and controlling behaviour, asserting that, 'Parties shall take the necessary legislative or other measures to ensure that the intentional conduct of seriously impairing a person's psychological integrity through coercion or threats is criminalised'. The fact that a specific obligation to criminalise coercive control is now expressly contained within a Council of Europe treaty clearly demonstrates the developments which have occurred in recent years regarding conceptualisations of domestic abuse.

Importantly, the ECtHR has likewise recognised the conceptualisation of domestic abuse as coercive control. In its judgment in *Volodina v. Russia*, the Court commented that,

> Ill-treatment must attain a minimum level of severity if it is to fall within the scope of Article 3 … Even in the absence of actual bodily harm or intense physical or mental suffering, treatment which humiliates or debases an individual, showing a lack of respect for or diminishing his or her human dignity, or which arouses feelings of fear, anguish or inferiority capable of breaking an individual's moral and physical resistance, may be characterised as degrading and also fall within the prohibition set forth in Article 3.[80]

The ECtHR was clearly of the view that the physical violence which the applicant had suffered reached the level of severity required to come within the ambit of Article 3. However, the Court also emphasised the psychological aspects of the abuse which the applicant had endured, and commented that, 'The feelings of fear, anxiety and powerlessness that the applicant must have experienced in connection with (the perpetrator's) controlling and coercive behaviour were sufficiently serious as to amount to inhuman treatment within the meaning of Article 3 of the Convention'.[81]

In *Volodina*, the ECtHR emphasised the important fact that domestic abuse is not only constituted by physical violence but involves broader patterns of coercive and controlling behaviour, and that forms of non-physical abuse can come within the ambit of Article 3. The explicit recognition that psychological abuse is sufficient to meet the necessary threshold of severity to engage Article 3, even in the absence of physical injury, is meritorious, and demonstrates the evolution which the Court's jurisprudence on domestic abuse has undergone. Such statements on the part of the ECtHR are far removed from the understanding of the Court's approach which was held by the state in *Valiuliene*. There is certainly no longer scope for a state to be of

80 Para. 73.
81 Para. 75.

the opinion that a violation of Article 3 will not be found due to an applicant's physical injuries being insufficiently severe.

Conclusion

In conclusion, therefore, conceptualisations of domestic abuse in the jurisprudence of the ECtHR on domestic abuse have certainly evolved greatly, from an approach whereby the Court tended to apply Article 8 in such cases to a situation whereby the use of Article 3 is commonplace.[82] The ECtHR has also demonstrated a clear awareness that domestic abuse is not only constituted by physical violence, and that coercive control and psychological abuse can come within the ambit of Article 3. Indeed, the debate has now become whether domestic abuse should be expressly conceptualised by the Court as torture. Such a finding could certainly constitute a very welcome development, as it would make a strong statement regarding the seriousness of domestic abuse. As Herring remarks, 'There is a particularly strong stigma attached to torture, less than that found in references to inhuman or degrading treatment',[83] and as Judge Pinto de Albuquerque commented in *Volodina*, 'If the State faces condemnation for allowing its women to be subjected to torture, the positive obligation to protect is even more stringent'.[84]

The issues surrounding conceptualisations on the part of the ECtHR of domestic abuse, which were explored in this chapter, all surround the Court's use of Article 3 in such cases. However, Chapter 3 develops the theme of the ECtHR's evolving conceptualisation of domestic abuse by focusing on the Court's approach to such abuse as a form of gender-based discrimination under Article 14.

82 In addition to the cases considered in this chapter, violations of Article 3 have also been found in cases such as *M.G. v. Turkey* (App. No. 646/10), judgment of 22 March 2016; *Bălşan v. Romania* (App No. 49645/09), judgment of 23 May 2017; *Talpis v. Italy* (App. No. 41237/14), judgment of 18 September 2017 (discussed in Chapters 3 and 4); *D.M.D. v. Romania* (App. No. 23022/13), judgment of 3 October 2017; *Buturugă v. Romania* (App. No. 56867/15), judgment of 10 February 2020 (discussed in Chapter 5); *De Giorgio v. Italy* (App. No. 23735/19), judgment of 16 June 2022; *M.S. v. Italy* (App. No. 32715/19), judgment of 7 July 2022; *A.E. v.Bulgaria* (App. No. 53891/20), judgment of 23 May 2023 (discussed in Chapter Three); and *Luca v. Moldova* (App. No. 55351/17), judgment of 17 October 2023 (discussed in Chapter 5).

83 Herring J., *Domestic Abuse and Human Rights*, 2020, Intersentia, Cambridge, at 64.

84 Separate Opinion of Judge Pinto de Albuquerque, joined by Judge Dedov, at para. 9.

3 Domestic Abuse as Gender-Based Discrimination

Chapter 3 develops the theme of the evolving conceptualisation of domestic abuse on the part of the ECtHR by focusing on the Court's approach to domestic abuse as a form of gender-based discrimination under Article 14 of the ECHR. The chapter begins by examining questions surrounding domestic abuse and gender, and discussing the conceptualisation by the CEDAW Committee of domestic abuse as gender-based discrimination, before focusing on the relevant jurisprudence of the ECtHR. The Court's use of Article 14 in cases involving domestic abuse has expanded greatly in recent years, which is reflective of the Court's increased use of this provision more generally. The ECtHR has very clearly framed domestic abuse as a form of gender-based discrimination, as is discussed in this chapter.

Domestic Abuse and Gender

Questions relating to gender and domestic abuse have raised a great deal of debate. It is, of course, accepted that both women and men can be victims of domestic abuse, and indeed that both women and men can be perpetrators of such abuse. However, as Burton remarks, 'Contradictory views about whether women are as likely as men to perpetrate violence against an intimate partner abound in the literature'.[1] Dobash and Dobash assert that women's violence against men differs substantially from men's violence against women in terms of the context and the consequences.[2] Women's violence often occurs in the context of self-defence, and the consequences of women's violence against men tend to be less severe. Essentially, 'Women's violence towards male intimate partners does not occur with the same frequency or ferocity as men's violence towards female intimate partners'.[3] Dobash and Dobash, therefore,

1 Burton M., *Legal Responses to Domestic Violence*, 2008, Routledge-Cavendish, Abingdon, at 5.
2 Dobash R.P. and Dobash R.E., 'Women's Violence to Men in Intimate Relationships: Working on a Puzzle' (2004) 44 *British Journal of Criminology* 324.
3 Burton, op. cit., at 6.

DOI: 10.4324/9781003493068-3

opine that in formulating policies, priority should be accorded to those which tackle men's violence against women.[4] Likewise, Chinkin remarks that, 'while men also experience domestic violence, it is more frequently inflicted upon women and has disparate economic and social consequences';[5] and Kimmell is of the view that, 'When sexual violence and violence by ex-spouses are considered, the evidence is overwhelming that gender asymmetry in domestic violence remains in full effect'.[6] Indeed Women's Aid goes so far as to state that, 'In the vast majority of cases (domestic abuse) is experienced by women and is perpetrated by men'.[7] Given that domestic abuse seems to affect women disproportionately, it appears that such abuse can correctly be conceptualised as a form of gender-based discrimination.

The view of domestic abuse as constituting gender-based discrimination is well established within the UN context.[8] As was discussed in Chapter 1, domestic abuse was officially recognised by the CEDAW Committee as constituting gender-based discrimination as far back as 1992 when the Committee issued its General Recommendation No. 19. This document stated that,

> The definition of discrimination includes gender-based violence, that is, violence that is directed against a woman because she is a woman or that affects women disproportionately … Gender-based violence may breach specific provisions of the Convention, regardless of whether those provisions expressly mention violence.[9]

General Recommendation No. 19 emphasised,

4 Dobash and Dobash, op. cit.

5 Chinkin C., 'Addressing violence against women in the Commonwealth within states' obligations under international law' (2014) 40 *Commonwealth Law Bulletin* 471 at 475.

6 Kimmel M.S., '"Gender Symmetry" in Domestic Violence: A Substantive and Methodological Research Review' (2002) 6 *Violence Against Women* 1332 at 1359. For further discussion of arguments surrounding 'gender symmetry' as regards domestic abuse, see Johnson M.P., 'Conflict and Control: Gender Symmetry and Asymmetry in Domestic Violence' (2006) 12 *Violence Against Women* 1003. For further discussion of domestic abuse as a gendered phenomenon, see Bishop C., 'Domestic Violence: The Limitations of a Legal Response' in Hilder S. and Bettinson V. (eds), *Domestic Violence – Interdisciplinary Perspectives on Protection, Prevention and Intervention*, 2016, Palgrave Macmillan, London, 59 at 61–62.

7 Women's Aid, 'What is domestic abuse?', https://www.womensaid.org.uk/information-support/what-is-domestic-abuse/.

8 Domestic abuse against men is, however, an important issue which should not be forgotten. For a discussion of domestic abuse against men, see Martin L., 'Debates of Difference: Male Victims of Domestic Violence and Abuse' in Hilder S. and Bettinson V. (eds), *Domestic Violence – Interdisciplinary Perspectives on Protection, Prevention and Intervention*, 2016, Palgrave Macmillan, London, 181.

9 UN Committee on the Elimination of Discrimination Against Women, 'General Recommendation No. 19: Violence against women' (1992), at para. 6.

> that discrimination under the Convention is not restricted to action by or on behalf of Governments ... Under general international law and specific human rights covenants, States may be responsible for private acts if they fail to act with due diligence to prevent violations of rights or to investigate and punish acts of violence, and for providing compensation.[10]

The General Recommendation also stated that,

> Family violence is one of the most insidious forms of violence against women. It is prevalent in all societies. Within family relationships women of all ages are subjected to violence of all kinds, including battering, rape, other forms of sexual assault, mental and other forms of violence, which are perpetuated by traditional attitudes.[11]

It can be seen, therefore, that in General Recommendation No. 19, the issue of domestic abuse was simply framed as a form of gender-based violence, which in turn was conceptualised as discrimination against women. Likewise, in its General Recommendation No. 35 on gender-based violence against women, which the CEDAW Committee issued in 2017 in order to update General Recommendation No. 19, the Committee stated very clearly that, 'Gender-based violence against women constitutes discrimination against women'.[12] As Chinkin comments, the CEDAW Committee has thus rejected the view that domestic abuse 'can be described in gender-neutral language that conceals the gender-based quality of violence against women'.[13]

Interestingly, the approach of the drafters of the Istanbul Convention differs to a certain extent from that of the CEDAW Committee in this regard. In Article 3(b) of the Istanbul Convention, 'domestic violence' is defined in a gender-neutral manner as encompassing 'all acts of physical, sexual, psychological or economic violence that occur within the family or domestic unit or between former or current spouses or partners, whether or not the perpetrator shares or has shared the same residence with the victim'. However, although Article 2(2) asserts that, 'Parties are encouraged to apply this Convention to all victims of domestic violence', this provision also states that, 'Parties shall pay particular attention to women victims of gender-based violence in implementing the provisions of this Convention'. In addition, it is asserted

10 At para. 9.

11 At para. 23.

12 UN Committee on the Elimination of Discrimination Against Women, 'General recommendation No. 35 on gender-based violence against women, updating general recommendation No. 19' (2017), at para. 21.

13 Chinkin C., 'Violence Against Women' in Freeman M.A., Chinkin C. and Rudolf B. (eds), *The UN Convention on the Elimination of All Forms of Discrimination Against Women – A Commentary*, 2012, Oxford University Press, Oxford, 443 at 452.

in Article 2(1) that, 'This Convention shall apply to all forms of violence against women, including domestic violence, which affects women disproportionately'. Thus, whilst states are 'encouraged' to apply the provisions of the Convention to male victims of domestic abuse, the focus remains primarily on the prevention of violence against women, encompassing *inter alia* such violence which takes place in the home. Therefore, whilst the drafters of the Istanbul Convention recognised that anyone can be a victim of domestic abuse, they were nevertheless of the view that domestic abuse affects women disproportionately and constitutes a form of gender-based violence. This conceptualisation of domestic abuse as gender-based violence is also shared by the ECtHR, as emphatically demonstrated by its jurisprudence on this issue.

The Jurisprudence of the ECtHR on Domestic Abuse and Article 14

Article 14 of the ECHR states that,

> The enjoyment of the rights and freedoms set forth in this Convention shall be secured without discrimination on any ground such as sex, race, colour, language, religion, political or other opinion, national or social origin, association with a national minority, property, birth or other status.

O'Connell, writing in 2009, commented that although Article 14 had been 'sometimes regarded as a Cinderella provision; the European Court of Human Rights ... not developing it to have significant "bite"',[14] nevertheless the Court had in recent years taken 'huge strides in its understanding' of this provision.[15] The increased use of Article 14 by the ECtHR generally was reflected in an upsurge in the use of Article 14 in cases involving domestic abuse, with the Court conceptualising such abuse as a form of gender-based discrimination.

The first domestic abuse case before the ECtHR in which an applicant chose to make an argument based on Article 14 was *Opuz v. Turkey*,[16] the facts of which were discussed in Chapter 2. In this case, the applicant demonstrated through statistical data that domestic abuse affected mainly women and that judicial passivity in Turkey created a climate conducive to such

14 O'Connell R., 'Cinderella Comes to the Ball: Art 14 and the Right to Non-Discrimination in the ECHR' (2009) 29 *Legal Studies* 211 at 212.

15 *Ibid.*, at 228.

16 (App. No. 33401/02), judgment of 9 September 2009. For further discussion of this case, see Burton M., 'The human rights of victims of domestic violence: *Opuz v. Turkey*' (2010) 22 *Child and Family Law Quarterly* 131; and Londono P., 'Developing Human Rights Principles in Cases of Gender-Based Violence: *Opuz v. Turkey* in the European Court of Human Rights' (2009) 9 *Human Rights Law Review* 662.

abuse. In finding a violation of Article 14 taken in conjunction with Articles 2 (the right to life) and 3 (the right to be free from torture or inhuman or degrading treatment), the ECtHR stated that,

> Bearing in mind … that the general and discriminatory judicial passivity in Turkey, albeit unintentional, mainly affected women, the Court considers that the violence suffered by the applicant and her mother may be regarded as gender-based violence which is a form of discrimination against women.[17]

An argument based on Article 14 was again raised in *A v. Croatia*,[18] the facts of which were also discussed in Chapter 2. However, the ECtHR declared in this case that the applicant's complaint under Article 14 was inadmissible, as she had not given sufficient evidence, such as reports or statistics, to prove that the practices adopted in Croatia in relation to domestic abuse were discriminatory.

Violations of Article 14 were then found in a number of domestic abuse cases against Moldova. *Eremia and Others v. Moldova*[19] concerned a complaint by Ms Eremia and her two daughters regarding the authorities' failure to protect them from the violent behaviour of their husband and father. The ECtHR held that, despite their knowledge of the abuse, the authorities had failed to take effective measures against Ms Eremia's husband, and had failed to protect Ms Eremia from further domestic abuse. There had therefore been a breach of Article 3 with respect of Ms Eremia. The Court also considered that, despite the detrimental psychological effects on her daughters of witnessing their father's violence against their mother, little or no action had been taken to prevent the recurrence of such behaviour. There had thus been a violation of Article 8 with respect of the two daughters. In addition, the ECtHR found that the authorities' attitude had amounted to condoning violence and had been discriminatory towards Ms Eremia as a woman. There had therefore been a violation of Article 14 taken in conjunction with Article 3. In finding the breach of Article 14, the Court referred to a report compiled by the UN Special Rapporteur on violence against women, its causes and consequences, which highlighted the high levels of domestic abuse in Moldova and which stated that discriminatory attitudes in society as a whole constituted a major contributory factor to the high prevalence of violence against women in the home.[20]

17 At para. 200.

18 (App. No. 55164/08), judgment of 14 October 2010.

19 (App. No. 3564/11), judgment of 28 May 2013.

20 Report of the Special Rapporteur on violence against women, its causes and consequences, Mission to the Republic of Moldova, Doc. A/HRC/11/6/Add.4, 8 May 2009. Violations of Article

In *M.G. v. Turkey*[21] the applicant had been subjected to domestic abuse during her marriage, and then to threats following her divorce. The ECtHR held that there had been a breach of Article 3. The Court found that the authorities had taken a passive attitude, given that criminal proceedings against the applicant's former husband had not been opened until more than five years and six months after the applicant had lodged a complaint and that the proceedings were apparently still pending at the time of the ECtHR's judgment. The Court also held that there had been a violation of Article 14 read in conjunction with Article 3, finding that after the applicant's divorce was pronounced in September 2007 and until the entry into force of a new law in March 2012, the legislative framework in place did not guarantee that the applicant, a divorcée, could benefit from protection measures. The ECtHR noted that for many years after applying to the national courts, the applicant had been forced to live in fear of her ex-husband's conduct.[22]

In *Talpis v. Italy*[23] the applicant had suffered from domestic abuse, which had resulted in the murder of her son and her own attempted murder. The ECtHR found that by failing to take prompt action on the complaint lodged by the applicant, the authorities had created a situation of impunity conducive to the recurrence of violence, which had led to the attempted murder of the applicant and the death of her son. There had thus been a violation of Article 2. The Court also held that there had been a breach of Article 3 due to the failure of the authorities in their duty to protect the applicant from domestic abuse. The ECtHR noted that the applicant had lived with her children in a climate of violence and that the manner in which the authorities had conducted the criminal proceedings indicated judicial passivity.

In addition, the ECtHR held that there had been a violation of Article 14 in conjunction with Articles 2 and 3, finding that the applicant had been the victim of discrimination as a woman on account of the inaction of the authorities, which had underestimated the violence in question and thus essentially endorsed it. The Court stated that 'by underestimating, through their complacency, the seriousness of the violent acts in question, the Italian authorities in effect condoned them'.[24] The ECtHR was of the view that the applicant had provided,

14 were also found in *Mudric v. Moldova* (App. No. 74839/10), judgment of 16 July 2013; *T.M. and C.M. v. Moldova* (App. No. 26608/11), judgment of 28 January 2014; *Munteanu v. Moldova* (App. No. 34168/11), judgment of 26 May 2020; and *Luca v. Moldova* (App. No. 55351/17), judgment of 17 October 2023.

21 (App. No. 646/10), judgment of 22 March 2016.

22 A violation of Article 14 was also found in *Halime Kilic v. Turkey*, (App. No. 63034/11), judgment of 28 June 2016.

23 (App. No. 41237/14), judgment of 2 March 2017.

24 At para. 145.

> prima facie evidence, backed up by undisputed statistical data, that domestic violence primarily affects women and that, despite the reforms implemented, a large number of women are murdered by their partners or former partners (femicide) and, secondly, that the socio-cultural attitudes of tolerance of domestic violence persist.[25]

The Court therefore considered that the abuse perpetrated against the applicant 'must be regarded as based on her sex and accordingly as a form of discrimination against women'.[26]

Interestingly, five years later in its judgment in *M.S. v. Italy*[27] which also involved domestic abuse, the ECtHR took note of the fact that since its judgment in *Talpis*, the state had taken steps to implement the Istanbul Convention, thereby demonstrating a genuine commitment to preventing and tackling violence against women. The Court was of the view that while there had been a breach of Article 3 due to the authorities' failure to act, this could not be deemed in itself to demonstrate a discriminatory attitude on the part of the authorities. The applicant's complaint under Article 14, taken in conjunction with Article 3, was thus declared to be inadmissible, as being manifestly ill-founded.

In *Balsan v. Romania*[28] the ECtHR held that there had been a breach of Article 3 due to the failure of the authorities to protect the applicant from her husband's violence, and also a violation of Article 14 in conjunction with Article 3. The Court noted that official statistics showed that domestic abuse was 'tolerated and perceived as normal by a majority of people' in the state and that 'a rather small number of reported incidents' were followed by criminal investigations.[29] The number of victims of such abuse had increased each year, with the vast majority of victims being women. In the view of the ECtHR, 'the authorities did not fully appreciate the seriousness and extent of the problem of domestic violence in Romania and … their actions reflected a discriminatory attitude towards the applicant as a woman'.[30] The Court considered that there was '*prima facie* evidence that domestic violence mainly affected women and that the general and discriminatory passivity of the authorities created a climate that was conducive to domestic violence'.[31] The ECtHR was of the opinion that the abuse suffered by the applicant could be regarded as 'gender-based violence, which is a form of discrimination against women', and that 'the overall unresponsiveness of the judicial system and the

25 At para. 145.
26 At para. 148.
27 (App. No. 32715/19), judgment of 7 July 2022.
28 (App. No. 49645/09), judgment of 23 May 2017.
29 At para. 83.
30 At para. 85.
31 At para. 86.

impunity enjoyed by aggressors, as found in the instant case … indicated that there was an insufficient commitment to take appropriate action to address domestic violence'.[32]

In *Volodina v. Russia*, the facts of which were discussed in Chapter 2, the ECtHR commented that, 'Substantive gender equality can only be achieved with a gender-sensitive interpretation and application of the Convention provisions that takes into account the factual inequalities between women and men and the way they impact women's lives'.[33] The ECtHR held that the evidence submitted by the applicant, along with information from international and domestic sources, was sufficient to establish *prima facie* indications that in Russia domestic abuse affected women disproportionately. However, the authorities had not adopted any legislation which was sufficient to provide protection to women who had been disproportionately affected by such abuse. The ECtHR therefore held that, in addition to a breach of Article 3, there had also been a violation of Article 14, taken in conjunction with Article 3.[34]

In *Tkhelidze v. Georgia*, a case in which the applicant's daughter had been killed as a result of domestic abuse and the facts of which are discussed further in Chapter 4, the ECtHR remarked that,

> the inactivity of the domestic law-enforcement authorities, in particular the police, appears to be even more unforgivable when assessed against the fact that, in general, violence against women, including domestic violence, has been reported to be a major systemic problem affecting society in the country at the material time.[35]

The authorities responsible thus 'knew or should have known of the gravity of the situation affecting many women in the country and should have thus shown particular diligence and provided heightened State protection to vulnerable members of that group'.[36] The ECtHR therefore concluded that 'the general and discriminatory passivity of the law-enforcement authorities in the face of allegations of domestic violence, of which the present case is a perfect illustration, created a climate conducive to a further proliferation of violence committed against women'.[37] The Court was of the view that,

32 At para. 88.

33 (App. No. 41261/17), judgment of 9 July 2019, at para. 111.

34 A violation of Article 14 was also found in *Tunikova and Others v. Russia*, ((App. Nos. 55974/16, 53118/17, 27484/18, 28011/19), judgment of 14 December 2021.

35 (App. No. 33056/17), judgment of 8 July 2021, at para. 56.

36 At para. 56.

37 At para. 56.

> the law-enforcement authorities demonstrated a persistent failure to take steps that could have had a real prospect of altering the tragic outcome or mitigating the harm. In flagrant disregard for the panoply of various protective measures that were directly available to them, the authorities failed to display special diligence to prevent gender-based violence against the applicant's daughter, which culminated in her death.[38]

It was therefore held that the state had breached Article 2, read in conjunction with Article 14.[39]

In *A.E. v. Bulgaria*,[40] the applicant, at the age of 15, had moved in with a 23-year-old man, who was referred to in the judgment as D.M. The applicant alleged that D.M. had been violent towards her on a regular basis. After one such attack, she went to hospital and was recorded as having injuries including extensive bruising which had been caused by blows from hard objects. The applicant's mother contacted social services, who in turn contacted the prosecutor's office. The prosecutor ordered that the police carry out a preliminary check into the complaints. The police interviewed the applicant and her mother, and the latter alleged that the applicant had been kicked and strangled by D.M. The prosecutor decided against opening criminal proceedings and found that only an offence subject to private prosecution, namely minor bodily harm, had been committed. The applicant attempted to have this decision overturned, but without success. The applicant argued, on the basis of Articles 3 and 14, that the state had failed to protect her from domestic abuse and to investigate sufficiently her complaints in this regard and that she had been discriminated against on the grounds of age and gender. The ECtHR held that the state had failed to put in place an effective system to punish all forms of domestic abuse and to provide adequate safeguards for victims. The state had not protected the applicant sufficiently, and there had thus been a breach of Article 3. The ECtHR also held that there had been a violation of Article 14 taken in conjunction with Article 3. The Court stated that 'violence against women, including domestic violence, is a form of discrimination against women, and that the State's failure to protect women from such violence breaches their right to equal protection of the law'.[41] The applicant had submitted statistics which established that women were the predominant victims of violence, including domestic abuse, in Bulgaria. The ECtHR asserted that,

38 At para. 57.

39 A violation of Article 14 was also found in *A and B v. Georgia*, (App. No. 73975/16), judgment of 10 February 2022.

40 (App. No. 53891/21), judgment of 23 May 2023. For discussion of this case, see McQuigg R., 'The Evolving Jurisprudence of the European Court of Human Rights on Domestic Abuse: *A.E. v. Bulgaria*', 27 June 2023, https://strasbourgobservers.com/2023/06/27/the-evolving-jurisprudence-of-the-european-court-of-human-rights-on-domestic-abuse-a-e-v-bulgaria/.

41 At para. 116.

> Taking into account that it is the applicant who bears the initial prima facie burden of proof of a difference in treatment, the Court is satisfied that the applicant has submitted sufficient statistical material … and has thus made a prima facie case that, by virtue of being a woman victim of domestic violence in Bulgaria, she was in an unequal position which required action on the part of the authorities in order to redress the disadvantage associated with her sex in that context.[42]

The Court proceeded to state that,

> once it has been established that domestic violence affects women disproportionately, it is for the Government to show what kind of remedial measures the domestic authorities have deployed to tackle that disadvantage and to ensure that women can fully enjoy human rights and freedoms on an equal footing with men.[43]

However, apart from general submissions, the state had not demonstrated what specific policies had been pursued with the aim of protecting victims of domestic abuse and punishing offenders. In the view of the ECtHR, the relevant legal provisions were not capable of responding sufficiently to domestic abuse, of which the majority of victims in Bulgaria were women. In addition, the Court found that the absence of official comprehensive statistics kept by the authorities could not be explained as a mere omission, 'given the level of the problem in Bulgaria and the authorities' related obligation to pay particular attention to the effects of domestic violence on women and to act accordingly'.[44] Also, the fact that the Bulgarian authorities had not ratified the Istanbul Convention could, in the view of the ECtHR, 'be seen as indicative of the level of their commitment to fighting effectively domestic violence'.[45] The Court therefore found that the authorities had not disproved the applicant's *prima facie* case of a general institutional passivity in matters related to domestic abuse. The ECtHR stated that,

> As the statistics provided by the applicant show, for a sustained period of time women have continued to suffer disproportionately from domestic violence and the authorities have not shown that they have engaged adequately with the problem. In such a case, it is not necessary for the

42 At para. 119.
43 At para. 119.
44 At para. 120.
45 At para. 121.

> applicant to show that she was individually a target of prejudice by the authorities.[46]

There had thus been a violation of Article 14, read in conjunction with Article 3.

Interestingly, findings of violations of Article 14 in domestic abuse cases have not been limited to circumstances involving failures on the part of agencies within the criminal justice systems of states. In *J.D. and A v. United Kingdom*,[47] the second applicant lived in a three-bedroom house in the social rented sector with her son. Under a 'Sanctuary Scheme', a 'panic room' had been installed in the attic due to the risk to her of domestic abuse from a man with whom she had had a brief relationship. A change to the rules on housing benefit (informally termed the 'bedroom tax') meant that the second applicant's housing benefit was reduced by 14 per cent, as the house was deemed to have one bedroom more than was necessary. The second applicant's housing benefit therefore no longer met the costs of her rent, and she was threatened with eviction, despite the fact that the house had been specially adapted. The second applicant argued that she had been discriminated against due to her situation as a victim of gender-based violence, and the ECtHR held that there had been a violation of Article 14, in conjunction with Article 1 of Protocol No. 1 (the right to protection of property).

In its judgment, the ECtHR emphasised that Article 14 does not only cover situations in which persons or groups are subjected to different treatment in cases in which such treatment would be discriminatory, but that this provision is also breached when states, 'without an objective and reasonable justification, fail to treat differently persons whose situations are significantly different'.[48] Article 14 therefore places positive obligations on states 'to make necessary distinctions between persons or groups whose circumstances are relevantly and significantly different'.[49] The Court proceeded to comment that,

> a policy or measure that has disproportionately prejudicial effects on a particular group may be considered discriminatory, regardless of whether the policy or measure is specifically aimed at that group. Thus, indirect discrimination prohibited under Article 14 may arise under circumstances where a policy or measure produces a particularly prejudicial impact on certain persons as a result of a protected ground, such as gender … attaching to their situation. In line with the general principles relating to the

46 At para. 122.
47 (App. Nos. 32949/17, 34614/17), judgment of 24 October 2019.
48 At para. 84.
49 At para. 84.

prohibition of discrimination, this is only the case, however, if such policy or measure has no 'objective and reasonable' justification.[50]

The ECtHR was of the view that the second applicant was particularly prejudiced by the measure in question because her situation was significantly different due to gender. All those whose housing benefits were reduced could risk losing their homes. However, the loss of her home could put the second applicant's personal safety at risk. Also, due to her vulnerable status, the second applicant did not have the same options available to her to mitigate her loss by, for example, taking in tenants, as did other recipients of housing benefits. The next question to be considered by the Court was therefore whether there was an objective and reasonable justification for the failure to take account of the difference in the second applicant's situation. The measure in question had the legitimate aim of curbing public expenditure by ensuring that social sector tenants of working age who were occupying premises with a greater number of bedrooms than needed should, where possible, move into smaller accommodation. The issue for the ECtHR was thus whether the treatment afforded to the second applicant 'was justified on the basis that there was a reasonable relationship of proportionality between the means employed and the aim sought to be realised'.[51] In considering this question, the Court noted that the legitimate aim of the measure was in conflict with the aim of Sanctuary Schemes, which was to enable those at serious risk of domestic abuse to stay in their own homes safely, and that the state had not given any weighty reasons to justify the prioritisation of the aim of the measure over that of such schemes. The ECtHR concluded that the imposition of the measure on those benefiting from Sanctuary Schemes had not been justified and was discriminatory. In doing so, the Court commented that, 'in the context of domestic violence … States have a duty to protect the physical and psychological integrity of an individual from threats by other persons, including in situations where an individual's right to the enjoyment of his or home free of violent disturbance is at stake'.[52] Following this judgment, the relevant Regulations[53] were amended[54] with effect from October 2021 to introduce an exemption from reduction in housing benefits for claimants whose homes had been adapted under a Sanctuary Scheme due to domestic abuse.

It is noteworthy that *J.D. and A v. United Kingdom* constitutes one of the few cases in the ECtHR's jurisprudence relating to domestic abuse which

50 At para. 85.

51 At para. 98.

52 At para. 105.

53 The Housing Benefit Regulations 2006 (SI 2006/213).

54 The Domestic Abuse Support (Relevant Accommodation and Housing Benefit and Universal Credit Sanctuary Schemes) (Amendment) Regulations 2021 (SI 2021/991).

addresses an issue other than criminal justice responses to such abuse. This is particularly important given that it has been argued that the most important needs of victims of domestic abuse are for social support measures, such as monetary resources, refuge accommodation and housing.[55] The rights contained in the ECHR largely fall within the category of 'civil and political' rights, as opposed to 'socio-economic' rights, as was referred to in Chapter 1, and there are generally limits on what courts can achieve. As Chayes comments, it is much more difficult for courts to order that affirmative programmes be put in place than it is for them to hold that a certain practice be halted.[56] Nevertheless, it is not impossible for courts to make such affirmative orders. Whilst it is unlikely that the ECtHR would hold specifically that refuges should be built, it is not inconceivable that it could order that steps should be taken to rehouse victims of abuse. In *Dulas v. Turkey*[57] the applicant had been forcibly evicted from her home by security forces. Her possessions were completely destroyed and she was forced to leave her village. The ECtHR held that the applicant's right to be free from inhuman or degrading treatment under Article 3 had been breached. As Paglione comments,

> women forced to abandon their homes by their violent partners and individuals forced to leave their homes by state agents are victims of the same process; they are coercively removed from their homes, chased away, and left without their possessions and with no alternative place to go.[58]

It is not impossible that the Court could hold that the rights of victims of domestic abuse are similarly violated if the state does not take sufficient steps to provide victims with accommodation. It is now well-recognised that the provision of social assistance is an important counter to domestic abuse. The ECtHR has repeatedly stated that the ECHR is a 'living instrument which … must be interpreted in the light of present-day conditions',[59] and as Mowbray comments, the Court has sought to apply the Convention rights 'in ways that provide genuine benefits to the 800 million persons falling within its jurisdiction'.[60]

55 For example, Schneider, E.M., *Battered Women and Feminist Lawmaking*, 2000, Yale University Press, London, at 52.

56 Chayes A., 'The Role of the Judge in Public Law Litigation', (1976) 89 *Harvard Law Review* 1281 at 1295–1296

57 (App. No. 25801/94), judgment of 30 January 2001.

58 Paglione G., 'Domestic Violence and Housing Rights: A Reinterpretation of the Right to Housing' (2006) 28 *Human Rights Quarterly* 120 at 139.

59 The Court first stated this principle in *Tyrer v. United Kingdom*, (App. No. 5856/72), judgment of 25 April 1978, at para. 31.

60 Mowbray A., 'The Creativity of the European Court of Human Rights' [2005] 5 *Human Rights Law Review* 57 at 79.

Conclusion

In conclusion, the ECtHR has very clearly conceptualised domestic abuse as a form of gender-based discrimination, and in doing so has followed the approach of UN bodies such as the CEDAW Committee in this respect. Essentially, once an applicant has brought forth evidence such as statistics to demonstrate that domestic abuse affects women disproportionately in the respondent state, it then falls upon the authorities to show that they deployed effective remedial measures to address that disadvantage. Should the state fail to demonstrate that such action has been taken, a violation of Article 14 will be found, as demonstrated by the relevant jurisprudence of the ECtHR to date.

Chapters 2 and 3 have focused on various aspects of how domestic abuse is conceptualised by the ECtHR. As explored particularly in Chapter 2, the way in which domestic abuse is framed by the Court has developed over the years, reflecting the Court's increasing understanding of such abuse. Chapter 4 analyses an important issue that has arisen in relation to the development of the Court's understanding of the dynamics of domestic abuse – namely, how the *Osman* test should be applied in this context.[61]

61 This test is derived from the judgment of the ECtHR in *Osman v. United Kingdom* (App. No. 23452/94), judgment of 28 October 1998.

4 Domestic Abuse and the '*Osman* Test'

A prominent theme in this book is the development of the ECtHR's understanding of domestic abuse. Chapter 4 analyses an important issue which has arisen in relation to this – namely, that of how the *Osman* test should be applied in the context of domestic abuse.[1] The first Grand Chamber judgment in a case focusing on such abuse was issued in *Kurt v. Austria* in June 2021.[2] In this judgment, the Grand Chamber set out a number of key principles that should be applied by the ECtHR when considering cases involving domestic abuse, particularly in the context of the right to life as found in Article 2 of the ECHR. Notably, the Grand Chamber addressed an important question that had arisen in previous cases as to how the *Osman* test should be applied in the context of domestic abuse. This test is derived from the judgment of the ECtHR in *Osman v. United Kingdom*[3] and is applied by the Court in all cases in which it is alleged that a state has failed to take appropriate steps to protect the right to life of an individual from the criminal acts of a third party. In *Osman,* it was established that in appropriate circumstances Article 2 entails a positive duty on the state to take preventive operational measures to protect an individual whose life is at risk from the criminal acts of another individual. However, for such a positive duty to arise, it must be established that the relevant authorities knew or ought to have known at the time of the existence of 'a real and immediate risk to the life of an identified individual'.[4]

Prior to the Grand Chamber's judgment in *Kurt v. Austria*, a recognition had begun to grow that the application of the *Osman* test in circumstances involving domestic abuse could be problematic, in terms of the need for the authorities to be aware of an 'immediate' risk to life in order for a positive duty

1 See also McQuigg R., 'Domestic Abuse and Article 2 of the European Convention on Human Rights: Applying the Grand Chamber Judgment in *Kurt v. Austria*' (2023) *European Human Rights Law Review* 564.

2 (App. No. 62903/15), judgment of 15 June 2021.

3 (App. No. 23452/94), judgment of 28 October 1998.

4 At para. 116.

DOI: 10.4324/9781003493068-4

to take preventive operational measures to arise.[5] In the context of domestic abuse, even if a risk to life does not appear to be immediate as such, there is a substantial possibility that it could escalate at any point. In *Kurt v. Austria*, the Grand Chamber established that the 'immediacy' element of the *Osman* test should be interpreted in such a manner as to take account of the specific nature of domestic abuse. It is argued that this judgment constitutes a landmark in the ECtHR's jurisprudence on domestic abuse. The Grand Chamber settled the questions which had arisen regarding how the *Osman* test should be applied in cases involving domestic abuse and indeed whether it should be used at all in such cases. It is now beyond doubt that, although the *Osman* test should be used, it must be applied in such a manner as to take account of the specific circumstances of domestic abuse. This is a welcome recognition, which demonstrates how the ECtHR's understanding of domestic abuse has increased and developed. However, it is also argued that the way in which the majority of the Grand Chamber proceeded to apply the very meritorious principles articulated in the first part of the judgment to the specific facts of the case in question is problematic. Having established that account must be taken of the particular circumstances of domestic abuse, it seems that the majority may then have failed to take these circumstances into consideration in a sufficient manner. The chapter includes a detailed discussion of the Grand Chamber's judgment and how the principles established therein have subsequently been applied by the ECtHR.[6]

The *Osman* Test in Domestic Abuse Cases Prior to *Kurt v. Austria*

Domestic abuse constitutes a substantial risk to the right to life. For example, in England and Wales, 373 domestic homicides were recorded by police during the three-year period ending March 2021. This represented approximately 20 per cent of all homicides where the victim was aged 16 or over during this period.[7] Prior to *Kurt v. Austria*, the ECtHR held in a significant number of cases that states had failed to take sufficient measures to protect the right

5 See, for example, *Valiuliene v. Lithuania* (App. No. 33234/07), judgment of 26 March 2013, Concurring Opinion of Judge Pinto de Albuquerque, at para. 31; *Volodina v. Russia* (App. No. 41261/17), judgment of 9 July 2019, Separate Opinion of Judge Pinto de Albuquerque, joined by Judge Dedov, at para. 12; and *Kurt v. Austria* (App. No. 62903/15), judgment of 4 July 2019 (first instance judgment), Concurring Opinion of Judge Huseynov, at paras. 3–4.

6 Relevant cases include *Tkhelidze v. Georgia* (App. No. 33056/17), judgment of 8 July 2021; *Y and Others v. Bulgaria* (App. No. 9077/18), judgment of 22 March 2022; and *Landi v. Italy* (App. No. 10929/19), judgment of 7 April 2022.

7 Office for National Statistics, 'Domestic abuse prevalence and trends, England and Wales: year ending March 2022', available at https://www.ons.gov.uk/peoplepopulationandcommunity/crimeandjustice/articles/domesticabuseprevalenceandtrendsenglandandwales/yearendingmarch2022.

to life in circumstances involving domestic abuse. Indeed it is notable that the first judgment of the ECtHR in which the issue of domestic abuse was addressed substantively involved a violation of Article 2 of the ECHR. In *Kontrova v. Slovakia*[8] the applicant, a victim of domestic abuse, argued that the police had failed to take appropriate action to protect her children's lives under Article 2 and her right to respect for her private and family life under Article 8, despite knowing of her husband's abusive behaviour. Her husband had threatened to kill himself and their two children, and he had ultimately carried out this threat. Under domestic law in Slovakia, the police had various specific duties such as accepting and registering the applicant's complaint, launching a criminal investigation and commencing proceedings against the applicant's husband immediately. However, they had failed to comply with any of these duties. The ECtHR held there had thus been a violation of Article 2 and that, in light of this finding, it was not necessary to also examine the case under Article 8. The ECtHR proceeded to find breaches of Article 2 in the domestic abuse cases of *Branko Tomasic and Others v. Croatia* in 2009;[9] *Opuz v. Turkey*, also in 2009;[10] *Durmaz v. Turkey* in 2014;[11] *Civek v. Turkey* in 2016;[12] *Halime Kilic v. Turkey*, also in 2016[13] and *Talpis v. Italy* in 2017.[14]

In all of these cases, the *Osman* test was applied. *Osman v. United Kingdom* involved a teacher who had wounded a student to whom he had developed an inappropriate attachment and who had also killed the student's father. Prior to this incident, he had carried out attacks on the family's property and threatened the deputy head teacher, who had expressed serious concerns regarding his behaviour. In its judgment in this case, the ECtHR stated that in certain circumstances, Article 2 places a positive duty on states to adopt preventive operational measures to protect an individual whose life is at risk from the criminal acts of another individual. However, in order for such a positive obligation to arise,

> it must be established that the authorities knew or ought to have known at the time of the existence of a real and immediate risk to the life of an identified individual from the criminal acts of a third party and that they failed to take measures within the scope of their powers which, judged reasonably, might have been expected to avoid that risk.[15]

8 (App. No. 7510/04), judgment of 31 May 2007.
9 (App. No. 46598/06), judgment of 15 January 2009.
10 (App. No. 33401/02), judgment of 9 June 2009.
11 (App. No. 3621/07), judgment of 13 November 2014.
12 (App. No. 55354/11), judgment of 23 February 2016.
13 (App. No. 63034/11), judgment of 28 June 2016.
14 (App. No. 41237/14), judgment of 2 March 2017.
15 (App. No. 23452/94), at para. 116.

In almost all of the domestic abuse cases involving alleged breaches of Article 2 which came before the ECtHR prior to *Kurt v. Austria*, applying the *Osman* test resulted in findings that the states in question had failed in their obligations under Article 2 to protect the lives of individuals from the actions of perpetrators of domestic abuse. An exception arose in the 2020 case of *Tershana v. Albania*,[16] in which the applicant suspected that her former husband, who had previously been abusive, had been behind an acid attack to which she had been subjected. She alleged that there had been a violation of Article 2 on the basis that the state authorities had failed to take measures to protect her from the attack. However, the ECtHR found that there had been no positive duty on the part of the state to take preventive operational measures in this instance as the national authorities had only found out about the violent behaviour of the applicant's former husband after the incident in question had taken place. The Court held, however, that there had been a breach of Article 2 in its procedural aspect, as the authorities had failed to conduct a prompt and effective investigation with the aim of identifying, prosecuting and punishing the applicant's assailant.

At first glance, therefore, use of the *Osman* test in Article 2 cases involving domestic abuse did not appear problematic, as the application of this test resulted in findings of violations in almost all such instances. Although a breach of Article 2 in its substantive aspect was not found in *Tershana*, this was unsurprising given that the state authorities had not been aware of abusive behaviour on the part of the applicant's former husband until after the incident in question had occurred. However, recognition had begun to grow that the application of the *Osman* test in some circumstances could be problematic, as 'over time the *Osman* test has been applied to a number of scenarios for which it was not originally conceived'.[17] Ebert and Sijniensky comment that,

> This would not be problematic if the different scenarios followed the inherent logic of the *Osman* case or if the Test was able to accommodate these scenarios in a satisfactory manner … (T)his is, however, not always the case. Rather, some of these scenarios differ significantly from that at stake in *Osman*, which sometimes renders the *Osman* Test's application unsuitable.[18]

Domestic abuse certainly constitutes a scenario that differs considerably from that which arose in the *Osman* case. As noted above, *Osman* involved a teacher

16 (App. No. 48756/14), judgment of 4 August 2020.

17 Ebert F.C. and Sijniensky R.I., 'Preventing Violations of the Right to Life in the European and Inter-American Human Rights Systems: From the *Osman* Test to a Coherent Doctrine on Risk Prevention?' (2015) 15 *Human Rights Law Review* 343 at 345.

18 Ebert and Sijniensky, op. cit., at 345.

who had injured a student and killed the student's father after having carried out attacks on the family's property and threatening the deputy head teacher. This scenario clearly differs greatly from the context of domestic abuse, in which even if the risk to life does not appear to be immediate as such, there is a substantial possibility that it could escalate at any point.

Although there had been little academic commentary on the difficulties surrounding the application of the *Osman* test to cases of domestic abuse, these problems had been the subject of judicial comment in a number of cases. For instance, although *Valiuliene v. Lithuania*,[19] a domestic abuse case of 2013 which was discussed in Chapter 2, involved Article 3 (the right to be free from torture or inhuman or degrading treatment or punishment) as opposed to Article 2, Judge Pinto de Albuquerque nevertheless commented regarding the *Osman* test in his concurring judgment that,

> Realistically speaking, at the stage of an 'immediate risk' to the victim it is often too late for the State to intervene. In addition, the recurrence and escalation inherent in most cases of domestic violence makes it somehow artificial, even deleterious, to require an immediacy of the risk. Even though the risk might not be imminent, it is already a serious risk when it is present.[20]

In *Volodina v. Russia*,[21] a 2019 domestic abuse case which was also discussed in Chapter 2 and which again involved a breach of Article 3, Judge Pinto de Albuquerque gave a separate opinion in which he further discussed this point, stating that,

> A 'real and immediate risk' in the context of domestic violence infers that the risk, namely the batterer, is already in the direct vicinity of the victim and about to strike the first blow. Were the test to be applied in such a manner, two concerns arise. Firstly, any protective action offered by the State would be too late and secondly, the State would have a legitimate excuse for not acting in a timely manner, since it is implausible to assume that the victim will be constantly accompanied by a State agent who may jump in to help. Hence, the 'immediacy' of the *Osman* test does not serve well in the context of domestic violence.[22]

19 (App. No. 33234/07), judgment of 26 March 2013.
20 (App. No. 33234/07) Concurring Opinion of Judge Pinto de Albuquerque, at para. 31.
21 (App. No. 41261/17), judgment of 9 July 2019.
22 Separate Opinion of Judge Pinto de Albuquerque, joined by Judge Dedov, at para. 12.

In the 2017 case of *Talpis v. Italy*,[23] which did involve Article 2, the ECtHR demonstrated some willingness to interpret the *Osman* test in such a manner as to take account of the specific circumstances involved in domestic abuse cases. The Court stated that, 'in judicial cases involving disputes relating to violence against women, the national authorities have a duty to examine the victim's situation of extreme psychological, physical and material insecurity and vulnerability and, with the utmost expedition, to assess the situation accordingly'.[24] The ECtHR also commented that, 'the risk of a real and immediate threat … must be assessed taking due account of the particular context of domestic violence. In such a situation it is not only a question of an obligation to afford general protection to society … but above all to take account of the recurrence of successive episodes of violence within the family unit'.[25] The judgment in this case seemed, therefore, to demonstrate some potential willingness on the part of the Court to apply the *Osman* test in such a manner as to take into consideration the particular nature of domestic abuse.

Nevertheless, even this limited recognition of the context of domestic abuse met with some opposition within the Court. A partly dissenting opinion was given by Judge Spano, in which he argued that the immediacy requirement of the *Osman* test had not been met and therefore the finding of a violation of Article 2 was not justified. In this case, the applicant had sought police assistance in June and August 2012 due to the violent behaviour of her husband and had lodged a complaint against him in September 2012, alleging bodily harm, ill-treatment and threats of violence. In November 2013, the applicant's husband attacked both the applicant and her son, resulting in the death of the latter. Due to the lapse of time between the events of June to September 2012 and the attack of November 2013, Judge Spano argued that 'it is plain that the requisite timeframe allowing for a conclusion of immediacy is lacking in the present case'.[26] Judge Spano proceeded to comment that,

> Regardless of how the judgment [in *Talpis*] frames it, the *Osman* test continues to apply in the same way here as in other contexts triggering the State's Article 2 preventive obligation; the Court's domestic violence case-law has continued to apply a strict *Osman* test without any alterations. Diluting the *Osman* standard, to take account of the nature of different types of fatal criminal offences between individuals, will simply impose an unrealistic burden on law enforcement authorities.[27]

23 (App. No. 41237/14), judgment of 18 September 2017.
24 At para. 130.
25 At para. 122.
26 Partly Dissenting Opinion of Judge Spano, at para. 5.
27 Partly Dissenting Opinion of Judge Spano, at para. 9.

The judge also stated that,

> Although it may be tempting to dilute legal concepts such as the *Osman* test when faced with heart-rending facts and give solace to individuals in situations such as that of the applicant, there are reasons why the threshold under the Convention is set high, and, in my view, why it must continue to remain so. Even in the field of domestic violence the ends cannot justify the means in a democratic society governed by the rule of law.[28]

It can be seen, therefore, that Judge Spano was very strongly opposed to views such as those expressed by Judge Huseynov in *Kurt* and Judge Pinto de Albuquerque in *Valiuliene* regarding the need to apply the *Osman* test in such a manner as to take account of the particular context of domestic abuse. However, the views of Judge Spano are somewhat unconvincing on this point. The *Osman* test is a judge-made concept – it is not found in the ECHR itself – and can thus be amended by the ECtHR as the Court sees fit. At the time when the *Osman* test was formulated, the view of domestic abuse as being a human rights issue was underdeveloped, and indeed it was not until almost a decade after its judgment in *Osman* that the ECtHR gave substantive consideration to the issue of domestic abuse. The Court repeatedly states that the ECHR is a 'living instrument which … must be interpreted in the light of present-day conditions'.[29] If this is the case, it seems rather strange to regard a test which has been formulated by the ECtHR as constituting an immutable concept. As discussed above, domestic abuse is a crime of a very particular nature, as pointed out by Judges Huseynov and Pinto de Albuquerque. Providing an effective response to domestic abuse requires law enforcement authorities to have an understanding of this context. In order to be effective in protecting victims of domestic abuse, it is essential for such authorities to take into consideration the nature of this type of potentially fatal criminal offence. Holding states to account for failing to do so cannot, therefore, be viewed as imposing 'an unrealistic burden on law enforcement authorities'.[30]

Given the emergence of such questions surrounding the application of the *Osman* test in domestic abuse cases, it would only be a matter of time before this issue would have to be directly addressed by the ECtHR.

28 Partly Dissenting Opinion of Judge Spano, at para. 16.

29 The ECtHR first stated this principle in *Tyrer v. United Kingdom*, (App. No. 5856/72), judgment of 25 April 1978, at para. 31.

30 Partly Dissenting Opinion of Judge Spano, at para. 9.

Kurt v. Austria

Such questions ultimately resulted in the referral of *Kurt v. Austria* to the Grand Chamber. In this case, the applicant alleged that the Austrian authorities had failed in their duties to protect her and her children (referred to in the judgment as A and B) from violence inflicted by her husband (referred to in the judgment as E), which had ultimately resulted in the death of her son. In July 2010 the applicant had informed the police that her husband had been violent towards her over a period of several years, and that recently the situation had worsened. The police noted that the applicant showed signs of injuries on her elbow and upper arm. In January 2011, E was convicted of committing bodily harm and dangerous threatening behaviour and was sentenced to three months' imprisonment, suspended for three years with probation.

On 22 May 2012, the applicant filed for divorce. In her hearing before the judge, she explained that the reasons for the breakdown of the marriage were her husband's violence and continuous threats. Later that day, the applicant reported E to the police for rape and for making dangerous threats. She stated that since February 2012, he had been threatening to kill her or to kill the children on a daily basis. The applicant said that she had not reported these threats at an earlier stage as she had been afraid that her husband would act upon them if she had done so. She reported that he was violent towards her on a regular basis, and was also violent towards the children. However, the situation had escalated on 19 May when the issue of a possible separation had arisen. During the course of the ensuing argument, E had repeatedly stated that he could not live without the applicant and the children, and had choked and raped her. The applicant stated that she was in great fear of her husband and that she had contacted the police because she wanted to protect both herself and her children.

Following this report, a police officer accompanied the applicant to the family home. E contested the allegations of violence; however, the children confirmed that he had regularly been violent towards them as well as towards their mother. A barring order was subsequently issued against E. This order obliged him to leave the home and prohibited him from returning either to it or to the surrounding areas, as well as barring him from the applicant's parents' apartment and its surrounding area. Also, his keys to the marital home were seized. Criminal proceedings were issued against E on the basis of the suspicion of rape, bodily harm and making dangerous threats.

On 25 May 2012, E went to the school which A and B attended. He asked A's teacher if he could speak briefly to A in private, and the teacher, who had not been informed of the issues within the family, agreed. A did not, however, return to class, and the teacher found him in the basement of the school, having been shot in the head. A was taken to hospital but died of his injuries two days later. E was found dead in his car, having committed suicide.

The applicant brought proceedings before the ECtHR, alleging that the Austrian authorities had failed to fulfil their positive obligations under Article 2 to protect her and her children from E. She argued that the state had failed to protect her son by not taking E into pre-trial detention. The legislative framework which had been in force in Austria at the relevant time had not allowed the police to extend barring orders to places other than residential premises, such as the children's school, and the applicant argued that this was a negligent omission which constituted a breach of Article 2. She also argued that after she had complained to the police in May 2012, it should have been obvious that there was a significant risk of E committing new acts of violence. The applicant had drawn the attention of the police to E's previous criminal convictions for threatening behaviour and bodily harm, his long history of violence against the applicant and her children, the evidence of injuries she had sustained, the threats E had been issuing since March 2012 and the very specific and continuous nature of these threats. Although the applicant had stated in her report to the police that she feared for her children's lives, the children had not been identified as endangered persons in the police report. Essentially, the applicant argued that the authorities had had sufficient information at hand to make them aware of the increased risk of further criminal offences by E against his family, but had failed to take effective preventive measures to protect A's life, in violation of Article 2.

However, in its judgment of 4 July 2019,[31] the ECtHR held unanimously that there had been no violation of Article 2.[32] The Court reiterated its oft-cited principle that Article 2 requires the state 'not only to refrain from the "intentional" taking of life, but also to take appropriate steps to safeguard the lives of those within its jurisdiction'.[33] This positive obligation encompasses a duty on the state to put in place a legislative and administrative framework designed to provide effective deterrence against threats to the right to life. Also, in appropriate circumstances, there is a positive obligation on the authorities to take preventive operational measures to protect an individual whose life is at risk from the criminal acts of another individual, as was established in *Osman*. In addition, the ECtHR pointed out that, 'Children and other vulnerable individuals in particular are entitled to State protection'.[34]

The ECtHR proceeded to set out the familiar principle, also established in *Osman*, that,

31 (App. No. 62903/15), judgment of 4 July 2019.

32 For further discussion of the first instance judgment, see McQuigg R., '*Kurt v. Austria*: Applying the *Osman* Test to Cases of Domestic Violence' (2020) *European Human Rights Law Review* 394.

33 At para. 62.

34 At para. 63.

> bearing in mind the difficulties involved in policing modern societies, the unpredictability of human conduct and the operational choices which must be made in terms of priorities and resources, the obligation to take preventive operational measures to protect an individual whose life is at risk from the criminal acts of another individual must be interpreted in a way which does not impose an impossible or disproportionate burden on the authorities. Accordingly, not every claimed risk to life can entail for the authorities a Convention requirement to take operational measures to prevent that risk from materialising.[35]

Indeed, for such a positive obligation to arise,

> it must be established that the authorities knew or ought to have known at the time of the existence of a real and immediate risk to the life of an identified individual from the criminal acts of a third party and that they failed to take measures within the scope of their powers which, judged reasonably, might have been expected to avoid that risk.[36]

Applying these principles to the instant case, the question for the ECtHR was therefore, had the Austrian authorities known or ought to have known of the existence of a real and immediate threat to the life of the applicant's children from the criminal acts of her husband, in respect of which they had failed to take appropriate measures?

The ECtHR pointed out that immediately following the applicant's report of domestic abuse in May 2012, the police had issued barring orders regarding the marital home and the applicant's parents' home. The Court was of the view that such barring orders would have been sufficient to protect the applicant and her children within these areas, especially as E had complied fully with such orders in 2010. Therefore, the question to be answered was whether the authorities could or should have known that the applicant's husband posed a real and immediate risk to his son's life outside of these areas, which could only have been averted by using pre-trial detention.

The ECtHR proceeded to set out the evidence that had been in the possession of the public prosecutor's office when deciding which measures to take against the applicant's husband. This included that he had a history of violence; two years previously, a barring order had been issued against him; and he had been convicted of causing bodily harm and uttering dangerous threats. Although the resulting sentence had been suspended, he was still within the three-year probationary period of that conviction, and there was strong

35 *Kurt*, at para. 64; *Osman*, at para. 116.
36 *Kurt*, at para. 65; *Osman*, at para. 116.

evidence that he had committed precisely the same offences again. There was physical evidence in the form of injuries to the applicant to support the allegations of bodily harm in 2012. In addition, the applicant had given a detailed account of the alleged rape to the police, while E's statements concerning this incident had contained a number of contradictions.

However, the ECtHR also pointed out in its judgment that before reporting the alleged rape, the applicant had spent three further days with E in the marital home. In addition, E's alleged violent outbursts prior to the killing of his son had been confined to the marital home, from which the Court said he had been effectively barred. Also, there had been no indications that E was in possession of a gun. When interviewed by police, E had appeared calm and had not given the impression of posing an immediate threat. In addition, the ECtHR noted that E had complied with the previous barring order, which had been made in 2010, and the authorities had not been informed of any further violence until the incidents of May 2012. In respect of the threats which E had made to kill his children, the Court noted that threats had allegedly been issued by E on a daily basis over a period of two months without these having been acted upon. The ECtHR therefore accepted the view of the state authorities that these threats did not indicate an immediate risk to the children's lives outside the home.

The domestic legislative framework had not allowed the police to extend barring orders to locations such as the children's school. In response to the applicant's argument that this was a negligent omission in breach of Article 2, the ECtHR reiterated that under the circumstances known to the authorities, a risk to the lives of the children while they were at school had not been discernible. The relevant domestic legislation had since been amended to allow for the issuing of barring orders in respect of schools and childcare facilities; however, the applicant's argument that the amendment of this legislation should be interpreted as a recognition of the alleged deficiency was, according to the Court, inconclusive. In the view of the ECtHR, 'An improvement made to a legal framework in the aftermath of a crime cannot be interpreted, as such, as recognition of a previous deficiency'.[37]

Finally, the ECtHR found it 'worth noting that the applicant herself seemed not to have been aware of the acute danger emanating from her husband in respect of their children following the incident reported on 22 May 2012', as she had remained in the marital home for three days following that incident before going to the authorities, and had not sought police protection at an earlier stage.[38] The Court therefore concluded that the state authorities had not failed to comply with their positive obligations and found that there had been no violation of Article 2.

37 At para. 78.
38 At para. 79.

However, a concurring opinion was issued by Judge Huseynov in which he agreed that it would be difficult to conclude that the Austrian authorities had failed in their positive obligations to protect the applicant's son, and he did not, therefore, dissent from the finding of no violation of Article 2. However, Judge Huseynov stated that what had prompted him to write a separate opinion was that 'in its judgment the Court has robustly applied the so-called *Osman* test to a domestic violence case', and that, 'Having done so, the Court has overlooked the peculiarity of domestic violence as a distinctive social phenomenon'.[39] In the judge's view, 'the relevance of this test is questionable in the particular context of domestic violence, that is to say, in cases where domestic violence has fatal results'.[40] Judge Huseynov proceeded to comment that,

> It is widely recognised that domestic violence often constitutes not just an isolated incident, but rather a continuous practice of intimidation and abuse. Therefore the State authorities should react, with due diligence, to each and every act of domestic violence and take all necessary measures to make sure that such acts do not lead to more serious consequences. It follows that the duty to prevent and protect comes into play when the risk to life is present, even if it is not imminent. In other words, in a domestic violence case, the positive obligation to protect life can be violated even where the risk to life is not immediate.[41]

Essentially, domestic abuse rarely consists of a single incident but usually comprises an ongoing cycle of abuse. Therefore, even if the risk to life in such a case does not seem to be immediate, there is a substantial possibility that it could escalate at any point, simply due to the nature of domestic abuse. Indeed, Judge Huseynov also commented that,

> seeking to prove the immediacy of the risk to life in domestic violence cases in order to establish a violation of Article 2 would not be consonant with the scope of the due-diligence obligations of States in the field of preventing and combating domestic violence particularly in the light of the Council of Europe's Convention on Preventing and Combating Violence against Women and Domestic Violence (the Istanbul Convention).[42]

Kurt v. Austria was then referred to the Grand Chamber, the majority of which agreed with the first instance judgment that there had been no violation of

39 Concurring Opinion of Judge Huseynov, at para. 1.
40 Concurring Opinion of Judge Huseynov, at para. 3.
41 Concurring Opinion of Judge Huseynov, at para. 4.
42 Concurring Opinion of Judge Huseynov, at para. 4.

Article 2 on the facts of the case.[43] It is notable however that, unlike the decision of the Chamber, the Grand Chamber's decision was far from unanimous, with the finding of no violation being made on the basis of ten votes to seven.

The Grand Chamber took the opportunity to set out in some detail the positive obligations of the state under Article 2 in the context of domestic abuse, and focused in particular on how the *Osman* test should be applied in such cases. In this regard, the Grand Chamber stated that, 'The existence of a real and immediate risk to life ... must be assessed taking due account of the particular context of domestic violence', and proceeded to clarify 'what it means to take into account the specific context and dynamics of domestic violence under the *Osman* test'.[44] Firstly, the Grand Chamber stated that 'an immediate response to allegations of domestic violence is required from the authorities',[45] and that 'special diligence is required from the authorities when dealing with cases of domestic violence'.[46] The judgment then noted that 'in order to be in a position to know whether there is a real and immediate risk to the life of a victim of domestic violence ... the authorities are under a duty to carry out a lethality risk assessment which is autonomous, proactive and comprehensive'.[47] In doing so, the authorities should 'not rely solely on the victim's perception of the risk, but ... complement it by their own assessment'.[48] The Grand Chamber emphasised the importance of regular training for authorities dealing with victims, in terms of understanding the dynamics of domestic abuse, thus enabling them to better assess any risk and to respond in an appropriate manner. Also, 'where several persons are affected by domestic violence, be it directly or indirectly, any risk assessment must be apt to systematically identify and address all the potential victims'.[49] In addition, 'the law-enforcement authorities should share information on risks and coordinate support with any other relevant stakeholders who come into regular contact with persons at risk, including, in the case of children, with teachers'.[50]

As regards the interpretation of the term 'immediate' in the *Osman* test, the Grand Chamber stated that 'the application of the immediacy standard in

43 (App. No. 62903/15), judgment of 15 June 2021. For further discussion of the Grand Chamber's judgment, see McQuigg R., '*Kurt v. Austria*: Domestic Violence Before the Grand Chamber of the European Court of Human Rights' (2021) *European Human Rights Law Review* 550. See also McQuigg R., 'The Evolving Jurisprudence of the European Court of Human Rights on Domestic Abuse' in Czech P., Herschl L., Lukas K., Nowak M. and Oberleitner G. (eds), *European Yearbook on Human Rights*, 2022, Intersentia, Cambridge, 205 at 217–224.

44 Grand Chamber judgment, at para. 164.

45 At para. 165.

46 At para. 166.

47 At para. 168.

48 At para. 169.

49 At para. 173.

50 At para. 174.

this context should take into account the specific features of domestic violence cases, and the ways in which they differ from incident-based situations' such as that which pertained in the *Osman* case itself.[51] In particular, 'consecutive cycles of domestic violence, often with an increase in frequency, intensity and danger over time, are frequently observed patterns in that context'.[52]

The Grand Chamber's detailed discussion of the application of the *Osman* test in cases involving domestic abuse is undoubtedly a welcome development. Although the Grand Chamber in *Kurt v. Austria* did not jettison the 'immediacy' element of the *Osman* test in situations of domestic abuse, it made it clear nevertheless that this element must be applied in such a way as to take account of the specific circumstances of such cases. This serves to clarify the approach of the Court in this respect and is certainly a meritorious development in the case law of the ECtHR on this issue. Indeed, it is noteworthy that Judge Spano was part of the majority in *Kurt v. Austria*, and therefore seemed no longer to subscribe to the views that he had articulated in *Talpis v. Italy*, as discussed earlier in this chapter.

If it is established that there is a real and immediate risk to the life of one or more identified individuals, the positive obligation on the part of the state authorities to take operational measures is then triggered. In this respect, the Grand Chamber asserted that, 'the toolbox of legal and operational measures available must give the authorities involved a range of sufficient measures to choose from, which are adequate and proportionate to the level of (lethal) risk that has been assessed'.[53] In particular, it noted that, 'If children are involved or found to be at risk, the child protection authorities should be informed as soon as possible, as well as schools and/or other childcare facilities'.[54]

Overall, the elaboration by the Grand Chamber of these general principles to be applied in cases involving domestic abuse is very much to be welcomed. It is meritorious that in so doing, the Grand Chamber referred to a significant degree to relevant provisions of the Istanbul Convention; the Explanatory Report on this instrument; and third-party comments which were received from the Istanbul Convention's primary monitoring body, the Group of Experts on Action Against Violence Against Women and Domestic Violence (GREVIO).[55] In particular, the fact that it has now been established beyond doubt by a Grand Chamber judgment that the 'immediacy' element of the *Osman* test should be interpreted in such a manner as to take account of the

51 At para. 175.
52 At para. 175.
53 At para. 168.
54 At para. 180.
55 'Third Party Intervention by the Group of Experts on Action against Violence against Women and Domestic Violence (GREVIO) pursuant to article 36 paragraph 2 of the European Convention on Human Rights: Application no. 62903/15 *Kurt v. Austria*', 21 January 2020, GREVIO/Inf(2020)3.

specific nature of domestic abuse serves to clarify the approach of the ECtHR in this respect and is certainly a meritorious development in the jurisprudence of the Court on this issue. It has now been firmly established that, although the *Osman* test should still be used in such cases, it must be applied in such a way as to take account of the particular circumstances of domestic abuse, as distinct from other types of criminality.

However, although the Grand Chamber appeared to be in unanimous agreement in terms of the articulation of the general principles that should be applied in cases involving domestic abuse, the Court was sharply divided on the question of how these principles should be applied to the facts of the case in question. Seven of the 17 judges disagreed with the finding of no violation of Article 2 and issued a joint dissenting opinion, in which they asserted that 'the risk assessment procedures in place were flawed in certain important respects', and that 'the assessment of the lethality risks was also inadequate as to its substance, as the authorities unjustifiably overemphasised certain factors and underemphasised others'.[56]

As the dissenting judges pointed out, the police had not been authorised to carry out any risk assessment beyond that which was made in order to ascertain whether a barring order should be issued. This required only a finding of a risk of further violence by the alleged perpetrator and did not consist of a comprehensive risk assessment focusing specifically on whether there were lethal risks to the family members.[57] In particular, no separate risk assessment was explicitly carried out regarding the children, and the authorities appeared to have focused exclusively on the applicant as the main target of E's violence and threats.[58]

The dissenting judges were of the view that elements which had been given too much emphasis included the fact that when the police had interviewed E, he had seemed to be calm and cooperative, and that he was courteous and friendly towards acquaintances.[59] However domestic abuse is an 'unseen crime' which takes place behind closed doors.[60] Frequently the perpetrators of this form of abuse will present themselves to the outside world as being calm and non-violent. Likewise, the Austrian authorities appeared to have adopted the view that as the violence had previously been confined to

56 Joint Dissenting Opinion of Judges Turković, Lemmens, Harutyunyan, Elósegui, Felici, Pavli and Yüksel, at para. 7.

57 Joint Dissenting Opinion of Judges Turković, Lemmens, Harutyunyan, Elósegui, Felici, Pavli and Yüksel, at para. 9.

58 Joint Dissenting Opinion of Judges Turković, Lemmens, Harutyunyan, Elósegui, Felici, Pavli and Yüksel, at para. 12.

59 Joint Dissenting Opinion of Judges Turković, Lemmens, Harutyunyan, Elósegui, Felici, Pavli and Yüksel, at para. 24.

60 See further McQuigg R., *International Human Rights Law and Domestic Violence*, 2011, Routledge, Abingdon, at 75–76.

the home, this meant that there was little risk of E being violent outside of the home. However, as the dissenting judges commented, 'Violence is person-dependent, not place-dependent'.[61] In addition, although the police checked whether there were any weapons registered in E's name, it seems that they did not ask the applicant herself about whether her husband had any weapons in his possession. The dissenting judges remarked that, 'Given the critical importance in the domestic violence context of determining whether a perpetrator has access to a weapon ... we do not consider that a simple check for weapons lawfully registered in the applicant's husband's name was sufficient'.[62] Also, it appeared that the authorities had placed too much emphasis on the fact that the applicant had not reported the alleged rape and strangulation by E until three days after the attack.[63] As noted above, domestic abuse is an 'unseen crime' which victims are often reluctant to report to the police. This reluctance may be for a number of reasons, including a fear of reprisals from the perpetrator. The fact that the applicant had remained in the marital home for three days cannot be taken as an indication of a lack of danger.

Aspects of the situation, which in the view of the dissenting judges were afforded insufficient emphasis by the authorities in the risk assessment, included the pattern of escalating violence endured by the applicant and her children. In particular, E had attempted to strangle the applicant and, as the dissenting judges noted, 'There is strong empirical evidence that attempted strangulation is a significant red flag'.[64] The authorities may also have afforded insufficient attention to the presence of a number of triggers of domestic homicide, such as the fact that the question of a divorce had arisen, with the possibility that E might lose custody of the children.[65] Indeed, it is often the case that the most dangerous time for a victim of domestic abuse is when she seeks to leave the relationship. In addition, it appeared that a number of risk factors had not been taken into account, such as E's gambling addiction, his economic dependence on the applicant and the applicant's job loss.[66]

Given that the majority of the Grand Chamber was of the view that the risk assessment was of a sufficient standard, they accepted that as the assessment had not indicated a real and immediate threat to the life of the applicant's son,

61 Joint Dissenting Opinion of Judges Turković, Lemmens, Harutyunyan, Elósegui, Felici, Pavli and Yüksel, at para. 25.

62 Joint Dissenting Opinion of Judges Turković, Lemmens, Harutyunyan, Elósegui, Felici, Pavli and Yüksel, at para. 15.

63 Joint Dissenting Opinion of Judges Turković, Lemmens, Harutyunyan, Elósegui, Felici, Pavli and Yüksel, at para. 27.

64 Joint Dissenting Opinion of Judges Turković, Lemmens, Harutyunyan, Elósegui, Felici, Pavli and Yüksel, at para. 20.

65 Joint Dissenting Opinion of Judges Turković, Lemmens, Harutyunyan, Elósegui, Felici, Pavli and Yüksel, at para. 21.

66 Joint Dissenting Opinion of Judges Turković, Lemmens, Harutyunyan, Elósegui, Felici, Pavli and Yüksel, at para. 11.

no obligation arose on the part of the authorities to take preventive operational measures. However, as discussed above, it is arguable that there were deficiencies in the risk assessment, and that a real and immediate threat engaging an obligation to take preventive measures should have been identified. If so, it would seem that the relevant legislative framework may not have been adequate. Essentially, at the time of the events in question, there was no requirement under Austrian law for information regarding domestic abuse to be shared with the children's school, and no possibility for the barring order to be extended to the school. Although the state argued that the applicant could have applied for a judicial temporary restraining order which could have extended to the school, the dissenting judges pointed out that the timeframe involved in the issuing of such an order would have been uncertain, and moreover, it was unacceptable that 'a victim of domestic violence who has reason to fear an imminent attack on the lives of her children should be required to pursue judicial proceedings in order to save their lives'.[67] It is also notable that, following the events in this case, the national legislation was amended to provide for the extension of police barring orders to schools as well as for the immediate notification in such cases of child protection authorities. In addition, as of January 2020, the relevant legislation was amended to provide for no-contact orders which follow the endangered person, as opposed to being confined to certain locations. As the dissenting judges commented, 'While such improvements cannot strictly be held against the respondent State with the benefit of hindsight, it is at the same time difficult not to see the multiple amendments undertaken since as implicit recognition at the national level of the flaws of the protective legal framework as it existed at the relevant time'.[68] The very fact that the law was amended due to the events which gave rise to this case could well be viewed as evidence demonstrating the inadequacy of the relevant legislative framework.

Indeed, the only protective measure that was adopted by the authorities was the barring order issued against E, which prevented him from entering the family home, the applicant's parents' home and the areas surrounding both. However, the fact that the order was limited to these locations undermined its effectiveness. In addition, as the dissenting judges stated, 'it is widely recognised in the domestic violence context that barring orders, in and of themselves, are not sufficient to prevent an attack on life, even if they mitigate the risk to some extent and should certainly be used as appropriate'.[69] If, contrary

67 Joint Dissenting Opinion of Judges Turković, Lemmens, Harutyunyan, Elósegui, Felici, Pavli and Yüksel, at para. 33.

68 Joint Dissenting Opinion of Judges Turković, Lemmens, Harutyunyan, Elósegui, Felici, Pavli and Yüksel, at para. 34.

69 Joint Dissenting Opinion of Judges Turković, Lemmens, Harutyunyan, Elósegui, Felici, Pavli and Yüksel, at para. 35.

to the majority judgment, it is accepted that the risk assessment was inadequate and that a real and immediate risk should have been identified, it seems that the measures adopted were insufficient to address this risk.

The majority judgment of the Grand Chamber in *Kurt v. Austria* certainly had significant merits. The first part of the judgment set out in a fairly detailed manner the principles that should be applied in cases involving domestic abuse. Prior to the Grand Chamber's judgment, questions had arisen in relation to how the *Osman* test should be applied in such cases, as discussed above, and the fact that this issue has now been clarified in a Grand Chamber judgment is to be welcomed. It has now been firmly established that, although the *Osman* test should still be used in such cases, it must be applied in such a manner as to take account of the particular circumstances of domestic abuse, as distinct from other types of criminality.

However, it is arguable that the way in which the majority of the Grand Chamber then proceeded to apply these principles to the specific facts of the case in question was problematic. Having established that account must be taken of the particular circumstances of domestic abuse, it seems that the majority may then have failed to take these circumstances into consideration in a sufficient manner. This is unfortunate due to the risk of undermining the very meritorious principles which were elaborated upon in the earlier part of the judgment. Indeed, according to the dissenting judges, 'The judgment … risks being seen as not taking sufficiently seriously the general principles laid out regarding risk assessment in cases of domestic violence'.[70] The Grand Chamber judgment in *Kurt v. Austria* certainly constituted a substantial development in the jurisprudence of the ECtHR on the issue of domestic abuse; however, it remained to be seen how the principles articulated therein would henceforth be applied by the Court.

Tkhelidze v. Georgia

Tkhelidze v. Georgia[71] was the first case involving domestic abuse in which judgment was issued by the ECtHR following the Grand Chamber judgment in *Kurt v. Austria*. In this case, the applicant's daughter, referred to in the judgment as M.T., moved into a flat with a man referred to in the judgment as L.M. in August 2013. The flat was also occupied by L.M.'s parents and M.T.'s daughter who was then aged six. In April 2014, L.M.'s father called the police to the flat as L.M. was abusing M.T. L.M.'s parents told the police that their son

70 Joint Dissenting Opinion of Judges Turković, Lemmens, Harutyunyan, Elósegui, Felici, Pavli and Yüksel, at para. 41.

71 (App. No. 33056/17), judgment of 8 July 2021. For further discussion of this case, see McQuigg R., '*Tkhelidze v. Georgia*: Domestic Abuse and the European Court of Human Rights' (2022) 11 *International Human Rights Law Review* 138.

suffered from pathological jealousy and became particularly aggressive while intoxicated. L.M.'s father also stated that his son's violent behaviour and death threats against M.T. were frightening and that he wanted the police to make L.M. leave the property. According to the police report, M.T. feared for her life and asked the police to take all measures necessary to prevent her partner from behaving in a similar way again. However, no criminal investigation was opened into the matter, and no restrictive measures were issued regarding L.M.

On 22 September 2014, M.T. contacted the police to say that L.M. had abused her, both physically and verbally. A police officer attended the scene and drew up a report stating that M.T. had been physically assaulted by her partner, in an act classified as criminal battery, and that she had consequently called an ambulance and received medical assistance. The report also stated that M.T. had been subjected to systematic verbal abuse and threats. The police officer questioned L.M., who admitted that he had made death threats against M.T. on multiple occasions. However, he told the officer that he would never harm or assault M.T. again. On the same date, M.T. was interviewed by an investigator from the criminal police unit. After the interview, the investigator issued a report which reclassified the incident as a less serious 'shove'. The police advised M.T. that it was not possible to arrest L.M. or for any other restrictive measure to be implemented, and again no investigation was opened.

M.T. then moved in with her mother (the applicant), whereupon L.M. began sending her messages in which he threatened to kill both M.T. and her young daughter. M.T. reported these threats to the police, and a police report stated that she asked the police to help her finally end the aggression. However, a police officer advised M.T. that no restrictive measures could be imposed in respect of L.M. as his violent behaviour had not been witnessed by the police.

On 27 September 2014, M.T. filed a criminal complaint against L.M. in relation to further threats against both herself and her daughter. In particular, she reported that the previous evening L.M. had attempted to break into the flat which was occupied by the applicant, M.T., and M.T.'s daughter, and had threatened to kill them and to set fire to M.T.'s car. L.M. was subsequently interviewed by the police. According to the interview record, he stated that he wished to reunite with M.T., and the police investigator then reclassified the reported death threats as verbal abuse. No criminal investigation was opened; however, a formal warning was given to L.M. to refrain from engaging in any type of dispute with M.T.

On 28 September 2014, M.T. was accosted by L.M. on her way home. She managed to reach her flat safely and immediately called the police. The police report stated that for the three previous days, M.T. had been receiving text messages containing death threats from L.M., regarding which she had already lodged a complaint. A police officer informed M.T. that L.M. could not be arrested for making threats in the absence of a physical assault.

Between late September and mid-October 2014, the applicant reported to the police on three occasions that L.M. had been stalking and threatening M.T. every day, and urged the police to provide protection. The applicant also reported that L.M. had once gone to her daughter's workplace with a hand grenade which he had threatened to detonate. However, the police took no action. On 15 October 2014, M.T. contacted the police, stating that L.M. had come to her workplace, and that she was extremely frightened of him. A police officer took a statement; however, no further steps were taken, and the police officer reiterated that an aggressor had to be caught 'red-handed' before an arrest could be made or any other restrictive measures could be imposed.

On 16 October 2014, M.T. again contacted the police and reported that while she had been driving to her daughter's school, she had been followed by L.M., who had attempted to stop her and had almost crashed into her car. Again, no further action was taken by the police. On the same day, the applicant reported to the police that her life and that of M.T. had become unbearable as L.M. had been terrorising them daily. The applicant stated that M.T. had been carrying defence pepper spray and a taser at all times. The applicant pleaded for protection; however, the police merely drew up another report. According to the various police reports, neither M.T. nor the applicant were at any time advised of their procedural rights or the legislative and administrative measures of protection that were available to them under national law. On 17 October 2014, L.M. went to M.T.'s workplace with a gun, shot her dead and then committed suicide.

An investigation was opened into the homicide and unlawful possession of a firearm by L.M. However, the investigation was discontinued in December 2014, the reason being that the person liable for the crime was deceased. In April 2015, the applicant filed a criminal complaint with the district public prosecutor's office, requesting that an investigation for negligence be opened against the police officers who had dealt with M.T.'s case. No reply was received, and so the applicant reiterated her complaint, further specifying that the inactivity of the police officers in question could amount to gender-based discrimination. The applicant lodged her complaint on at least four occasions between August and December 2015 for the attention of either the Chief Public Prosecutor's Office, which was the authority competent to launch criminal inquiries against police officers, or the General Inspectorate of the Ministry of the Interior (MIA), which was the unit in charge of disciplinary supervision of those working for the Ministry. The Chief Public Prosecutor's Office did not reply to the applicant's complaints; however, the MIA replied in January 2016, stating that it had no general jurisdiction to open an investigation into a crime allegedly committed by its officials without the consent of the Chief Public Prosecutor. In September 2016, the applicant's representative again contacted the Chief Public Prosecutor's Office requesting that a criminal investigation be launched against the police officers in question; however, no reply was received. In April 2017, the applicant enquired of the Chief Public Prosecutor's Office as to whether it had received her complaints and the reasons for the lack of response. The Chief Prosecutor's Office subsequently confirmed that it had received the complaints but still did not provide any response to these.

The applicant argued before the ECtHR that the state had failed to fulfil its positive obligations to protect the right to life of M.T. under Article 2 of the ECHR, and that the state had also violated the Article 14 non-discrimination provision. She alleged that, despite being aware of the danger posed to M.T.'s life by L.M.'s violent behaviour, the police had failed to take the necessary preventive measures. The applicant complained that they had insufficiently and inaccurately gathered and recorded evidence when dealing with the allegations of domestic abuse, and also that the relevant authorities had failed to investigate the circumstances which had contributed to M.T.'s death and to hold all those involved criminally responsible.

Following consideration of the facts of the case, the ECtHR held that there had been a violation of Article 2, in both its substantive and procedural aspects, taken in conjunction with Article 14. The Court, citing the judgment of the Grand Chamber in *Kurt*, stated that, 'Whenever there are any doubts about the occurrence of domestic violence or violence against women, an immediate response and further special diligence is required of the authorities to deal with the specific nature of the violence in the course of the domestic proceedings'.[72] The ECtHR commented that it was satisfied that there existed in Georgia an adequate legislative and administrative framework designed to combat domestic abuse. However, the manner in which this framework had been implemented by the law enforcement authorities raised 'serious concerns'.[73] Citing the Grand Chamber's judgment in *Kurt*, the Court identified three questions to be addressed in assessing this matter – 'whether a real and immediate danger emanating from an identifiable individual existed, whether the domestic authorities knew or ought to have known of the threat, and, should the above two questions be answered in the affirmative, whether the authorities displayed special diligence in their response to the threat'.[74]

In relation to the first two of these questions, the ECtHR noted that within a period of around six months, M.T. and the applicant had requested assistance from the police at least 11 times. On each of these occasions, they had clearly explained the level of violence involved in L.M.'s conduct. L.M. himself had admitted that he had been threatening to kill M.T., and his parents had confirmed to the police the dangerousness of their son's behaviour. In addition, the police knew that L.M. suffered from pathological jealousy, and that M.T. experienced extreme fear at seeing L.M. approaching either her home or

72 At para. 48.
73 At para. 52.
74 At para. 52.

her workplace. The ECtHR stated that, 'Where there is a lasting situation of domestic violence, there can hardly be any doubt about the immediacy of the danger posed to the victim',[75] and concluded that the police knew or ought to have known of the real and immediate threat to M.T.'s safety.

As regards the requirement of special diligence, which had been emphasised by the Grand Chamber in *Kurt*, the ECtHR identified a number of substantial failings on the part of the authorities. Firstly, there were indications of inaccurate or incomplete evidence-gathering by the police. In this regard, the Court commented that,

> shortcomings in the gathering of evidence in response to a reported incident of domestic violence can result in an underestimation of the level of violence actually committed, can have deleterious effects on the prospects of opening a criminal investigation and even discourage victims of domestic abuse, who are often already under pressure from society not to do so, from reporting an abusive family member to the authorities in the future.[76]

Citing the Grand Chamber's judgment in *Kurt*, the ECtHR stated that, 'It is also significant in this connection that, when recording the incidents, the police officers do not appear to have conducted a "lethality risk assessment" in an autonomous, proactive and comprehensive manner'.[77] The police did not attach sufficient importance to potential trigger factors, such as L.M.'s pathological jealousy further fuelled by the fact that he and M.T. had separated, and failed to take into account M.T.'s extreme fear. In addition, although the domestic legislative framework provided for the issuing of protective and restraining orders and for the possibility of isolating the abuser in a special rehabilitation centre, the police did not consider such options. Likewise, the police failed to advise M.T. of her procedural rights and of the various legislative and administrative measures of protection that were available. Indeed, it seemed that M.T. was misled by the police referring to their inability to arrest the abuser or to apply any other restrictive measures. The Court was of the view that there was, in fact, plenty of evidence that would have warranted the institution of criminal proceedings against L.M., thus opening up the possibility of pre-trial detention. According to the ECtHR, it was 'deplorable that the law-enforcement authorities did not do so'.[78]

The Court proceeded to comment that,

75 At para. 53.
76 At para. 54.
77 At para. 54.
78 At para. 55.

> the inactivity of the domestic law-enforcement authorities, in particular the police, appears to be even more unforgivable when assessed against the fact that, in general, violence against women, including domestic violence, has been reported to be a major systemic problem affecting society in the country at the material time.[79]

The authorities responsible, therefore, 'knew or should have known of the gravity of the situation affecting many women in the country and should have thus shown particular diligence and provided heightened State protection to vulnerable members of that group'.[80] The ECtHR thus concluded that 'the general and discriminatory passivity of the law-enforcement authorities in the face of allegations of domestic violence, of which the present case is a perfect illustration, created a climate conducive to a further proliferation of violence committed against women'.[81]

The Court asserted that,

> the law-enforcement authorities demonstrated a persistent failure to take steps that could have had a real prospect of altering the tragic outcome or mitigating the harm. In flagrant disregard for the panoply of various protective measures that were directly available to them, the authorities failed to display special diligence to prevent gender-based violence against the applicant's daughter, which culminated in her death.[82]

It was therefore held that the state had violated its substantive positive obligations under Article 2, read in conjunction with Article 14.

It can be seen, therefore, that the ECtHR in *Tkhelidze* certainly made use of the principles which had been laid out by the Grand Chamber in *Kurt*, particularly in terms of the need for 'special diligence' in responding to cases of domestic abuse and the necessity for a lethality risk assessment to be carried out in an autonomous, proactive, and comprehensive manner. However, it is worth noting that the facts of *Tkhelidze* demonstrated particularly major failings, which were described by the ECtHR as 'deplorable'[83] and 'unforgivable'.[84] Even if the *Osman* test had been applied in the traditional manner in this case, a violation of Article 2 would doubtless still have been found.[85]

79 At para. 56.
80 At para. 56.
81 At para. 56.
82 At para. 57.
83 At para. 55.
84 At para. 56.
85 A violation of Article 2 was also found in another domestic abuse case against Georgia – *A and B v. Georgia*, (App. No. 73975/16), judgment of 10 February 2022.

Y and Others v. Bulgaria

However, on 22 March 2022, the ECtHR issued its judgment in *Y and Others v. Bulgaria*,[86] another domestic abuse case in which the Court found a breach of Article 2. *Y and Others* involved arguably less extreme failures than those which were in question in *Tkhelidze* and thus demonstrates more clearly the impact of the Grand Chamber's judgment in *Kurt*. Indeed, it is arguable that had the judgment in *Y and Others* been issued prior to that of the Grand Chamber, a violation of Article 2 may not have been found.

In *Y and Others v. Bulgaria*, the first applicant's daughter (referred to in the judgment as Mrs V) had been killed by her husband (referred to in the judgment as Mr V). In 2014 Mr and Mrs V had stopped living together, and Mrs V had moved into her mother's flat. In November 2016, Mrs V reported to the police that the tyres of her car had been slashed, and that she suspected that Mr V had been the perpetrator. She explained that she and Mr V had had an argument ten days previously during which he had threatened to kill her, that Mr V owned a gun, and that she feared for her life. Upon being questioned by the police, Mr V denied slashing the tyres and, given that there had been no eyewitnesses to the incident, no criminal proceedings were issued. In January 2017, the first applicant made an emergency call stating that Mr V had come to the flat and was acting aggressively. Police officers arrived on the scene and reported that they had not witnessed an argument, but that they had cautioned the first applicant and Mr V to act lawfully and to resolve any disputes between them through proper legal channels. In February 2017, Mrs V complained to the police that, following an argument, her husband had pursued her, first by car and then on foot. She had met with him in his car at his request to discuss their daughters. Mr V was summoned to the police station and cautioned to refrain from making threats or being violent towards his wife. Mrs V then applied for a protection order, and the District Court issued an interim order the following day. Under the terms of the order, Mr V was barred from coming within 100 metres of his wife. A final protection order was issued in June 2017, under which Mr V was ordered to refrain from acts of domestic violence against Mrs V, and was barred for one year from coming within 100 metres of his wife, her home and her places of leisure.

On the evening of 17 August 2017, Mrs V made an emergency call stating that her husband was in breach of the protection order and that he was driving behind her car. She then told the call handler that her husband had disappeared from view. The call handler advised Mrs V to lodge a written complaint with the police, which she did that evening. The next day, Mrs V also lodged a

86 (App. No. 9077/18), judgment of 22 March 2022. For further discussion of *Y and Others v. Bulgaria*, see McQuigg R., 'The *Osman* Test in the Context of Domestic Abuse: *Y and Others v. Bulgaria*' (2022) *European Human Rights Law Review* 501.

complaint with the district prosecutor's office, stating that her husband owned a gun and that she feared for her life. After leaving the district prosecutor's office, Mrs V went to a coffee shop, whereupon her husband appeared and shot her five times. Mrs V died instantly.

In considering whether there had been a violation of Article 2, the ECtHR summarised the principles which had been set out by the Grand Chamber in *Kurt* as regards the scope of the duties placed on state authorities in the context of domestic abuse. Firstly, the authorities must respond immediately to allegations of such abuse. Secondly, when such allegations come to their attention, the authorities must carry out 'an autonomous, proactive and comprehensive risk assessment'[87] in order to check whether there is a real and immediate risk to life. In so doing, they must 'take due account of the special context of domestic violence when evaluating the risk's reality and immediacy'.[88] If it is found that such a risk to life exists, the authorities must take preventive operational measures which should be sufficient and proportionate to the assessed level of the risk.

In applying these principles to the facts of the case, the ECtHR stated that the only occasion on which the police responded immediately was in relation to the incident in January 2017. As regards the quality of the risk assessment which had been carried out, the ECtHR stated that there was nothing to suggest that the police had analysed Mr V's conduct in terms of what it could indicate regarding his future conduct. Rather, the police seemed only to have been concerned with the question of whether Mr V's acts should result in a public prosecution and appeared to have handled his wife's complaints without appreciating that the allegations suggested that the case 'concerned the special context of domestic violence and its typical dynamics'.[89] However, even assuming that an informal risk assessment had been carried out, such an assessment had not been 'autonomous, proactive or comprehensive'.[90] In particular, there was no evidence that, following Mrs V's complaint of November 2016 in which she mentioned that her husband had a gun, the police had checked whether he was in possession of such a weapon or whether he had a firearms licence. Referring to the judgment in *Kurt*, the ECtHR stated that, 'In the context of domestic violence, death threats should always be taken seriously and assessed as to their credibility'.[91] However, the police had not paid any attention to the death threats which Mrs V had reported in November 2016.

87 At para. 89.
88 At para. 89.
89 At para. 98.
90 At para. 99.
91 At para. 101, citing *Kurt*, Grand Chamber judgment, at para. 200.

In terms of whether the authorities knew or ought to have known that there was a real and immediate risk to the life of Mrs V, the ECtHR was of the view that had a proper risk assessment been carried out, it was likely that the authorities would have appreciated,

> that Mr V., who was alleged to have access to a handgun and had been repeatedly displaying the signs of an angry, violent and obsessive attitude towards Mrs V., could pose a real and immediate risk to her life, as those notions are to be understood in the context of domestic violence.[92]

Referring to the requirement for police officers to be 'specifically trained on the dynamics of domestic violence' as stipulated in *Kurt*,[93] the Court opined that the fact that the authorities had not appreciated the risk to Mrs V's life seemed to have been due at least partly to the lack of such training of the officers involved.

In relation to whether the authorities took preventive measures that were adequate under the circumstances, the ECtHR stated that the only operational measures taken to protect Mrs V were the interim and final protection orders. However, the interim order was not acted upon by the police department in charge of enforcing it, and it seemed that the final order was not brought to the attention of the police. The Court concluded that the authorities should have known on 17 August 2017 at the latest of a real and immediate risk to Mrs V's life, and that they failed to take any measures at their disposal which, judged reasonably, might have been expected to avoid that risk. The ECtHR also referred to the Grand Chamber's comment in *Kurt* that an effective preventive response frequently necessitates coordination between various authorities, and pointed out that there was no evidence to show that the authorities sought to coordinate their actions.[94] For example, it seemed that the district prosecutor's office had not attempted immediately to contact the police when it received Mrs V's complaint of 18 August.

The Court concluded that there had been a violation of Article 2.

The judgment in *Y and Others* constitutes a clear demonstration of the importance of the principles laid down by the Grand Chamber in *Kurt* for the jurisprudence of the ECtHR on domestic abuse. In its judgment in *Y and Others*, the Court cited *Kurt* extensively and indeed structured its entire analysis of whether there had been a breach of Article 2 around the principles which had been set out by the Grand Chamber. Moreover, it is arguable that in the absence of these principles, a violation may not have been found. Although it cannot be concluded for certain that a different decision would have been

92 At para. 105.
93 At para. 105, citing *Kurt*, Grand Chamber judgment, at para. 172.
94 At para. 109, citing *Kurt*, Grand Chamber judgment, at para. 180.

reached if the judgment in *Y and Others* had been issued prior to that of the Grand Chamber in *Kurt*, it is possible that a breach of Article 2 may not have been found using the *Osman* test in its traditional form. In *Y and Others*, the ECtHR frequently referred to the context of domestic abuse, and if the facts of the case are taken out of this context, it is debatable whether the Court would have held that the authorities should have been aware of a real and immediate risk to life. In particular, prior to the murder of his wife, it seems that Mr V had not actually engaged in physical violence towards her. It is, of course, crucial to bear in mind that domestic abuse does not consist solely of physical violence and may involve wider patterns of coercive control, as was discussed in Chapter 2. However, if the context of domestic abuse is removed from the case, it is debatable whether the authorities should have been aware of a real and immediate risk to life. The complaints made to the police could be said to have been small in number and only three of them related to incidents involving Mrs V (as the incident of 1 January 2017 involved the first applicant rather than Mrs V herself).

The first of these complaints involved the tyres of a car being slashed, and allegations of death threats having been made ten days previously. However, given that there were no eyewitnesses or evidence from surveillance cameras, the decision to take no further action beyond questioning Mr V may have seemed reasonable in the absence of the domestic abuse context. It appears that the failure to comply with the principles set out in *Kurt* regarding the need to carry out a speedy and comprehensive investigation of all allegations of domestic abuse, and the requirement for death threats always to be taken seriously in domestic abuse cases, were crucial to the Court's analysis of the authorities' response to this complaint.

The second complaint made by Mrs V related to her husband pursuing her, first by car and then on foot. Mr V was summoned to the police station and, despite denying having threatened his wife physically, was cautioned to refrain from making threats or being violent towards her. Whilst it could certainly be argued that charges should have been brought against Mr V, if this incident were taken out of a domestic abuse context again it may not indicate a 'real and immediate risk' to life, particularly as there was no actual physical violence involved and the victim had voluntarily met with the perpetrator in his car prior to the incident, which could be said to demonstrate a lack of fear on her part.

Mrs V made her third complaint at around 7:00 pm on the evening prior to her death. Again, there was no physical violence involved, and the complaint related to Mr V following his wife by car. If taken out of the domestic abuse context, it appears that the incident may not indicate a 'real and immediate risk' to life. The complaint which Mrs V made to the district prosecutor's office was lodged only around one hour before her death, and if removed from the context of domestic abuse it may have been reasonable for no action to have been taken within this time period. However, again the failure to comply with the principle set out in *Kurt* that the authorities must respond immediately to allegations of domestic abuse was significant, as was the failure of the district prosecutor's office to attempt immediately to contact the police, given the Grand Chamber's statement that an effective preventive response frequently necessitates coordination between various authorities.

Y and Others v. Bulgaria clearly demonstrates the importance of the Grand Chamber's judgment in *Kurt v. Austria.* In *Y and Others,* the ECtHR made extensive reference to the Grand Chamber's judgment, and indeed structured its analysis of the applicability of Article 2 around the principles set out by the Grand Chamber. It seems that there is a distinct possibility that the Court may well have arrived at a different conclusion in *Y and Others* if the *Osman* test in its traditional form had been applied, and that no breach of Article 2 would have been found. Overall, *Y and Others* constitutes a clear demonstration of the impact of the Grand Chamber's landmark judgment in *Kurt* on the case law of the ECtHR on domestic abuse.

Landi v. Italy

A month after the judgment of the ECtHR in *Y and Others*, the Court issued its judgment in *Landi v. Italy*.[95] In this case, the applicant had been attacked on four occasions by her partner (referred to in the judgment as N.P.). Proceedings had been commenced against N.P. on charges of domestic violence, but no orders had been issued for the protection of the applicant and her children. During the fourth attack, N.P. stabbed both the applicant and her son, causing his death.

In considering the case, the ECtHR again referred to the principles which had been set out by the Grand Chamber in *Kurt v. Austria,* whereby, firstly, the state authorities must react immediately to allegations of domestic abuse. Secondly, where such allegations are brought to their attention, the authorities must establish whether there is a real and immediate risk to life. In so doing, the authorities must carry out a risk assessment which is autonomous, proactive and exhaustive, and must take due account of the context of domestic abuse. Thirdly, if such a risk is identified, the authorities must take preventive operational measures which should be adequate and proportionate to the level of the risk identified.

In applying these principles, the ECtHR found that the authorities had failed to react immediately to the allegations of domestic abuse made by the applicant. They had also failed to conduct an immediate and proactive assessment of the risk of the recurrence of the violent acts committed against the applicant and her children, and to adopt preventative operational measures to

95 (App. No. 10929/19), judgment of 7 April 2022. This judgment is available in French only.

mitigate the risk and to protect those concerned. The authorities had known, or should have known, of a real and imminent risk to the lives of the applicant and her children. They should therefore have assessed the risk of further violence and taken appropriate and adequate action to protect the applicant and her children. In particular, public prosecutors had remained passive despite the serious risk involved, and their inaction had enabled the applicant's partner to continue to attack her with impunity. The authorities could have implemented protective measures by alerting the social services and placing the applicant and her children in a refuge; however, they had failed to do so. The ECtHR therefore held that the state authorities had failed in their positive duties to protect the lives of the applicant and her son, and that there had thus been a breach of Article 2.

It is, of course very possible that the ECtHR would have found a violation of Article 2 in *Landi v. Italy* even if the judgment in this case had been issued prior to that of the Grand Chamber in *Kurt v. Austria*. Nevertheless, as with *Tkhelidze v. Georgia* and *Y and Others v. Bulgaria*, the judgment in *Landi v. Italy* again serves to demonstrate that henceforth the ECtHR will approach domestic abuse cases involving Article 2 through the lens of the principles set out in *Kurt* – namely, the need for authorities to react immediately to allegations of such abuse; the need to carry out an autonomous, proactive and comprehensive assessment to establish whether there is a real and immediate risk to life, taking into account of the domestic abuse context; and, should such a risk be identified, the need to take adequate and proportionate preventive operational measures.

Conclusion

In conclusion, the judgment of the Grand Chamber in *Kurt v. Austria* certainly constitutes a landmark in the jurisprudence of the ECtHR on domestic abuse, particularly regarding the Court's use of Article 2 in such cases. Interestingly, the judgment may not result in changes to the ultimate outcomes in many cases. Even before the Grand Chamber's judgment, the ECtHR found violations in almost all of the domestic abuse cases in which the state's positive obligations under Article 2 were at issue, and *Kurt v. Austria* itself was one of the very few such cases in which no breach was found. However, the Grand Chamber's judgment settles the questions that had arisen regarding how the *Osman* test should be applied in cases involving domestic abuse and whether it should be used at all in such cases. It is now beyond doubt that, although the *Osman* test should be used, it must be applied in such a manner as to take account of the specific circumstances of domestic abuse. This is a welcome recognition, which demonstrates how the ECtHR's understanding of domestic abuse has increased and developed.

However, it is arguable that the way in which the majority of the Grand Chamber proceeded to apply the very meritorious principles articulated in the first part of the judgment to the specific facts of the case in question is problematic. Having established that account must be taken of the particular circumstances of domestic abuse, it seems that the majority may then have failed to take these circumstances into consideration in a sufficient manner. It appears that the dissenting judges may have had a better understanding of the dynamics of domestic abuse than that of their colleagues in the majority.

Nevertheless, it seems from the judgments that have since been issued by the ECtHR that henceforth the principles set out by the Grand Chamber will generally be followed closely by the Court in domestic abuse cases involving Article 2, thus potentially leading to a more uniform approach being taken by the ECtHR in its consideration of such cases. Also, the application of these principles could lead to the Court finding violations in circumstances in which it would not have done so prior to the Grand Chamber's judgment, as may have been the case in *Y and Others v. Bulgaria*. The jurisprudence of the ECtHR on Article 2 in the context of domestic abuse has certainly evolved greatly during a relatively short timeframe.

Chapter 5 focuses on a number of issues that have arisen in the ECtHR's very recent jurisprudence on domestic abuse, such as child contact in this context. Given that the early case law of the ECtHR on domestic abuse focused almost exclusively on the responses of police and prosecutors, the fact that this body of jurisprudence has now reached a stage whereby it encompasses detailed consideration of a specific matter such as child contact again demonstrates the extent to which the Court's understanding of the issue of domestic abuse has now developed.

5 Recent Issues in the Jurisprudence of the ECtHR on Domestic Abuse

Chapter 5 focuses a number of issues that have arisen in the very recent jurisprudence of the ECtHR on domestic abuse, which have been addressed under Article 8 of the ECHR, the right to respect for private and family life. As discussed in Chapter 2, Article 8 was used more extensively in the Court's earlier jurisprudence on domestic abuse;[1] and the ECtHR now makes more use of Article 3, the right to be free from torture or inhuman or degrading treatment, in such cases. Indeed, when addressing the responses of criminal justice systems to domestic abuse, the ECtHR almost always now bases its findings on either Article 3 or the right to life under Article 2, as well as frequently finding a breach of Article 14, the non-discrimination provision, as discussed in Chapter 3. However, the Court has found breaches of Article 8 in the recent cases of *Buturugă v. Romania*[2] and *Volodina v. Russia (No. 2)*,[3] both of which involved the very current issue of cyberviolence. In recent times there has been a growing recognition of the ways in which perpetrators may use technology in their abuse, and the chapter considers the ECtHR's approach to this issue.

Also, whilst the Court's early case law on domestic abuse focused almost exclusively on the responses of criminal justice systems, this body of jurisprudence has now evolved to encompass other aspects of state responses to such abuse. For example, in *Levchuk v. Ukraine*[4] a breach of Article 8 was found in circumstances in which a victim of domestic abuse complained that the domestic courts had refused to order the eviction of her former husband from

1 For example, *Bevacqua and S v. Bulgaria* (App. No. 71127/01), judgment of 12 June 2008; *A v. Croatia* (App. No. 55164/08), judgment of 14 October 2010; and *Kalucza v. Hungary* (App. No. 57693/10), judgment of 24 April 2012.

2 (App. No. 56867/15), judgment of 11 February 2020. A violation of Article 3 was also found in this case.

3 (App. No. 40419/19), judgment of 14 September 2021.

4 (App. No. 17496/19), judgment of 3 September 2020.

DOI: 10.4324/9781003493068-5

a flat which they occupied. Likewise, violations of Article 8 have been found in *I.M. and Others v. Italy*[5] and *Luca v. Moldova*,[6] both of which related to issues surrounding child contact in the context of domestic abuse. Given that the early case law of the ECtHR on such abuse focused almost exclusively on the responses of police and prosecutors, it is argued that the fact that this body of jurisprudence has now reached a stage whereby it encompasses detailed consideration of a specific matter such as child contact again demonstrates the extent to which the Court's understanding of the issue of domestic abuse has now developed.

The Decline in the Use by the ECtHR of Article 8 in Domestic Abuse Cases

As discussed in Chapter 2, in earlier cases involving domestic abuse in which applicants submitted arguments in respect of Articles 3 and 8, the ECtHR tended to base its findings of violations on Article 8. For example, breaches of this provision were found in *Bevacqua and S v. Bulgaria*[7] in 2008, *A v. Croatia*[8] in 2010 and *Kalucza v. Hungary*[9] in 2012. One possible explanation for this approach may be that, in the past, the ECtHR may not have fully appreciated the seriousness of domestic abuse and thus felt that it was more appropriate to deal with such cases as involving violations of the right to respect for private and family life, as opposed to the non-derogable right to be free from torture or inhuman or degrading treatment. However, the more likely explanation relates to very practical considerations. The ECtHR has an extremely heavy caseload and therefore frequently takes the approach of finding a violation of one provision of the ECHR and then omitting to consider the application of other provisions on which arguments have been made. The fact that, in domestic abuse cases, the ECtHR seemed to display a preference for the use of Article 8 over that of Article 3 may simply have been due to the fact that it can be easier to establish a breach of Article 8 than it is to establish a violation of Article 3.

However, if the reason for the Court's approach was simply expediency, the difficulty was that such an approach risked being interpreted as an approach based on principle, with that principle being that domestic abuse was only serious enough to fall within Article 8 but did not in the majority of cases, meet the threshold of constituting a violation of Article 3. Indeed, this seemed to be the understanding of the ECtHR's approach, which was held by

5 (App. No. 25426/20), judgment of 10 November 2022.
6 (App. No. 55351/17), judgment of 17 October 2023.
7 (App. No.71127/01), judgment of 12 June 2008.
8 (App. No. 55164/08), judgment of 14 October 2010.
9 (App. No. 57693/10), judgment of 24 April 2012.

the state in *Valiuliene v. Lithuania,*[10] as discussed in Chapter 2, in which the state submitted a unilateral declaration admitting a violation of Article 8 in circumstances involving domestic abuse but stating that the applicant's injuries were insufficiently serious to justify a finding of a breach of Article 3. The ECtHR responded by rejecting the unilateral declaration, holding that Article 3 had been violated and stating that it was therefore unnecessary to examine the case under Article 8. Interestingly, there is no explanation in the Court's judgment as to how this case differed from previous cases involving domestic abuse in which the ECtHR had found breaches of Article 8 and stated that it was not, therefore, necessary to also examine the cases under Article 3. Notably, Judge Jociene gave a Dissenting Opinion in *Valiuliene* in which she expressed the view that 'the Court has incorrectly relied on Article 3 in the circumstances of the present case' and that '[t]his position of the Chamber is not supported by the Court's case-law, where domestic violence cases are mostly examined from the perspective of Article 8 of the Convention'.[11] Judge Jociene proceeded to say that

> [a]ccordingly, and referring to the Court's case-law on the subject … the applicant's complaint in connection with the physical attacks on her should have been examined under Article 8 of the Convention and the applicant's right to respect for her private life.[12]

It seemed that by submitting the unilateral declaration, the state demonstrated that this was also its understanding of the Court's approach, and that by rejecting this declaration, the majority of the ECtHR wished to distance themselves from such an interpretation.

As discussed in Chapter 2, since the decision of the ECtHR in *Valiuliene*, the ECtHR has certainly made considerably more use of Article 3 in cases involving domestic abuse. Indeed, when addressing the responses of criminal justice systems to domestic abuse, the Court almost always now bases its findings on either Article 3 or the right to life under Article 2, as well as frequently finding a violation of Article 14, as was discussed in Chapter 3. However, the ECtHR has in recent times found violations of Article 8 in cases on the very current issue of cyberviolence in the domestic abuse context and in cases focusing on other aspects of state responses to such abuse, such as issues surrounding child contact in the context of domestic abuse.

10 (App. No.33234/07), judgment of 26 March 2013.
11 Dissenting Judgment of Judge Jociene, at para. 10.
12 Dissenting Judgment of Judge Jociene, at para. 11.

Cyberviolence

In recent times, there has been a growing recognition of the ways in which perpetrators of gender-based violence may use technology in their abuse.[13] For example, the Group of Experts on Action against Violence against Women and Domestic Violence (GREVIO), which constitutes one of the monitoring bodies of the Istanbul Convention, chose the digital dimension of violence against women as the subject of its first General Recommendation, which was adopted on 20 October 2021.[14] In this General Recommendation, GREVIO stated that it regarded 'the perpetration of violence against women online or with the help of technology as a continuity of the different forms of such violence that affects and exacerbates women and girls' experiences of gender-based violence against women to an alarming extent'.[15] GREVIO proceeded to comment that, 'Gender-based violence against women perpetrated in the digital sphere has a serious impact on women's and girls' lives, including psychological and physical health, their livelihoods, their physical safety and their reputation'.[16] Likewise, the European Union (EU) Directive on combating violence against women and domestic violence, which was adopted on 14 May 2024,[17] places obligations on EU member states to ensure the criminalisation of certain forms of cyberviolence, namely non-consensual sharing of intimate or manipulated material,[18] cyberstalking,[19] cyberharassment[20] and cyberincitement to violence or hatred.[21]

Importantly, cyberviolence has also now been recognised by the ECtHR. In *Buturugă v. Romania*[22] the applicant had lodged complaints against her husband, alleging that she had been the victim of domestic abuse and that her husband had threatened to kill her. The couple then divorced, following which the applicant requested an electronic search of the family computer, as she alleged that her former husband had wrongfully consulted her electronic accounts and had copied her private documents, conversations and

13 See McQuigg R, 'The Evolving Jurisprudence of the European Court of Human Rights on Domestic Abuse' in Czech P., Herschl L., Lukas K., Nowak M. and Oberleitner G. (eds), *European Yearbook on Human Rights*, 2022, Intersentia, Cambridge, 205 at 214–216.

14 Group of Experts on Action against Violence against Women and Domestic Violence, General Recommendation No. 1 on the digital dimension of violence against women, adopted on 20 October 2021. For a discussion of the monitoring mechanisms of the Istanbul Convention, see McQuigg R., *The Istanbul Convention, Domestic Violence and Human Rights*, 2017, Routledge, Abingdon, 110–136.

15 At para. 10.

16 At para. 12.

17 Directive 2024/1385.

18 Article 5.

19 Article 6.

20 Article 7.

21 Article 8.

22 (App. No. 56867/15), judgment of 11 February 2020.

photographs. She later lodged a further complaint of breach of the confidentiality of her correspondence. However, the prosecutor's office discontinued the case on the basis that the behaviour of the applicant's former husband had not been sufficiently serious to constitute a criminal offence. It also dismissed, as out of time, the applicant's complaint relating to the violation of the confidentiality of her correspondence, and imposed an administrative fine of around 250 euros on the applicant's former husband. The applicant appealed to a court, which issued her a protection order; however, she alleged that the police delayed the implementation of the order and that her former husband did not comply with it.

The ECtHR held that there had been breaches of both Articles 3 and 8. Essentially, the authorities had not addressed the case from the angle of domestic abuse and had based their decisions on the provisions of the criminal code, which penalised violence between private individuals, as opposed to those which provided for more stringent penalties for domestic abuse. In relation to the investigation into the breach of confidentiality, the ECtHR emphasised that cyberbullying constituted a recognised aspect of violence against women and girls, and that acts such as illicitly accessing one's partner's correspondence could be taken into account by the national authorities when investigating cases involving domestic abuse. However, the authorities had not considered the merits of the applicant's criminal complaint of violation of the confidentiality of her correspondence. The request which she had made for an electronic search of the family computer had been dismissed on the basis that any facts ascertained in this way would not be relevant to her former husband's alleged violence and threats. In addition, the domestic court had decided that the applicant's complaint relating to the alleged violation of the confidentiality of her correspondence was not pertinent to the subject matter of the case. The ECtHR was therefore of the view that the applicant's allegations relating to the use by her former husband of her electronic communications had not been examined on their merits, and that the state had failed to take into account the many forms in which domestic abuse can occur. The state had thus failed in its positive duties under Articles 3 and 8.

The issue of cyberviolence was also considered by the ECtHR in *Volodina v. Russia (No.2)*.[23] The circumstances were as set out in the discussion of *Volodina v. Russia*[24] in Chapter 2; however, the applicant took a second case before the ECtHR focusing in this instance on the online aspects of the abuse she had suffered. In June 2016, the applicant's brother informed her that her account on the Russian social media platform 'VKontakte' had been hacked. The invented name she had had on her account had been replaced with her real name, personal details had been added and a photograph of her passport,

23 (App. No. 40419/19), judgment of 14 September 2021.

24 (App. No.41261/17), judgment of 9 July 2019.

along with other photographs, had been uploaded. On attempting to log into her account, the applicant discovered that the password had been changed. She complained to the police, who then took a statement from the applicant's brother. He said that the applicant's former partner had admitted to him that he had hacked into her email account. At first, the police declined to institute criminal proceedings; however, a criminal investigation was eventually opened in March 2018. In September 2018, the applicant asked the investigator to seek an order which would prevent her former partner from using the internet, contacting her in any way, or approaching her or members of her family; however, this request was refused. In December 2018, the applicant complained to the Kuntsevskiy District Court in Moscow that the police had not responded in any way to her report that she had found a tracking device in her bag two years previously; however, the District Court found no fault with the actions of the police. In January 2019, the police suspended the investigation into fake social media profiles, and in September 2019, the police refused to open a criminal investigation into the tracking device. In October 2020, the police closed the criminal case. It had, however, been established that in February and March 2018 the applicant's former partner had created fake profiles on VKontakte in her name and had published nude photographs of her without her consent.

In its judgment, the ECtHR stated that,

> Online violence, or cyberviolence, is closely linked with offline, or 'real-life', violence and falls to be considered as another facet of the complex phenomenon of domestic violence … The States have a positive obligation to establish and apply effectively a system punishing all forms of domestic violence and to provide sufficient safeguards for the victims … The positive obligation applies to all forms of domestic violence, whether occurring offline or online.[25]

It was clear that there had been an interference with the applicant's rights under Article 8, due to the creation of fake social media profiles, the publication of her intimate photographs without her consent and her tracking by means of a GPS device. The question to be addressed was therefore whether the authorities, once they became aware of the interference with the applicant's Article 8 rights, had discharged their duties to take sufficient measures to stop the interference and prevent it from recurring. The ECtHR concluded that the existing legal framework did equip the authorities with tools to prosecute the acts in question. However, the manner in which the matter was handled, particularly in terms of the reluctance to open a criminal case and

25 At para. 49.

the slow pace of the investigation, demonstrated a failure on the part of the authorities to discharge their positive duties under Article 8 of the ECHR. There had thus been a breach of that provision.

The recognition on the part of the ECtHR that cyberviolence may constitute an aspect of domestic abuse is very welcome. Previously, UN human rights entities had recognised the part which online abuse can play in domestic abuse. For example, in 2015 the UN Human Rights Council asserted that domestic abuse can include cyberbullying and cyberstalking;[26] and in 2018 the UN Special Rapporteur on violence against women, its causes and consequences, stated that online abuse may form part of a pattern of domestic violence and abuse.[27] The fact that cyberviolence has also now been recognised by the ECtHR as a form of domestic abuse is certainly meritorious.

Levchuk v. Ukraine

Whilst the ECtHR's early case law on domestic abuse focused almost exclusively on the responses of criminal justice systems, this body of jurisprudence has now evolved to encompass other aspects of state responses to such abuse, as was discussed in Chapter 3, in relation to the Court's judgment in *J.D. and A v. United Kingdom*.[28] A further example of such development can be seen in *Levchuk v. Ukraine*,[29] in which the applicant, a victim of domestic abuse, complained that the domestic courts had refused to order the eviction of her former husband from a flat which they occupied with their three children and the applicant's son. The applicant had lodged a civil action under domestic legislation which provided for the possibility to evict tenants in social housing for systematic misconduct. Initially, a court had found in her favour, but this ruling was reversed in appeal proceedings, essentially on the basis that the eviction of the applicant's former husband would constitute a disproportionate interference with his right to respect for his home. The applicant did not object to the quality of the general response of the national authorities to her complaints of domestic abuse, but she argued that the courts' refusal to order the eviction had exposed her and the children to the risk of further victimisation.

In its judgment, the ECtHR stated that 'where an individual makes a credible assertion of having been subjected to repeated acts of domestic violence … it falls on the domestic authorities to assess the situation in its entirety,

26 Resolution adopted by the Human Rights Council on 2 July 2015, A/HRC/RES/29/14, at para. 4.

27 Report of the Special Rapporteur on violence against women, its causes and consequences on online violence against women and girls from a human rights perspective, 18 June 2018, A/HRC/38/47, at para. 31.

28 (App. Nos. 32949/17, 34614/17), judgment of 24 October 2019.

29 (App. No. 17496/19), judgment of 3 September 2020.

including the risk that similar incidents would continue'.[30] The Court proceeded to assert that,

> Where it is established that a particular individual has been systematically targeted and future abuse is likely to follow, apart from responses to specific incidents, the authorities may be called upon to implement an appropriate action of a general nature to combat the underlying problem and prevent future ill-treatment.[31]

The applicant had made 'credible assertions that over a prolonged period of time she had been exposed to physical assaults, intimidation and threats'[32] from her former husband, with whom she still shared a flat. The ECtHR stated that, 'These events affected her physical and mental integrity, and they therefore pertain to the sphere of private life within the meaning of Article 8 of the Convention … They likewise affected her right to the enjoyment of a home free from violent disturbance also protected under Article 8'.[33]

According to the ECtHR, although 'eviction is the most extreme measure of interference with one's right to respect for the home guaranteed by Article 8', nevertheless 'interference by the national authorities with individual rights under Article 8 might be necessary in order to protect the health and rights of the others'.[34] In particular, in cases involving domestic abuse, 'perpetrators' rights cannot supersede victims' human rights, in particular, to physical and mental integrity'.[35] The national courts, in the context of the eviction proceedings, had a duty to assess the credibility of the applicant's statements and the risk of future abuse should the parties remain living together in the flat. However, it was not apparent that a comprehensive assessment of these aspects had been performed, and indeed the proceedings had lasted for over two years, during which time the applicant and her children remained at risk of further abuse. A fair balance between all of the competing interests at stake had not therefore been struck, and the response of the domestic courts to the applicant's eviction claim against her former husband had not been in compliance with the state's positive obligation to ensure that the applicant was effectively protected from domestic abuse. There had thus been a violation of Article 8.

As noted in Chapter 3, it has been argued that the most important needs of victims of domestic abuse are social support measures, such as monetary

30 At para. 80.
31 At para. 80.
32 At para. 81.
33 At para. 81.
34 At para. 84.
35 At para. 84.

resources, refuge accommodation and housing.[36] Although the judgment in *Levchuk* related to ensuring the eviction of a perpetrator of domestic abuse, as opposed to ensuring that a victim was provided with alternative accommodation, the key issue was nevertheless ensuring the safety of the victim in terms of her housing arrangements. Whilst it is unlikely that the ECtHR would hold specifically that, for example, refuges should be built, it is certainly not inconceivable that the Court could order that steps should be taken to rehouse victims of abuse.

Child Contact

Another issue relating to state responses to domestic abuse, beyond criminal justice processes, which the ECtHR has now considered, is that of child contact against a background of domestic abuse. Such situations can raise difficult and varying issues. As Macdonald comments, 'child contact with the domestic violence perpetrator has been highlighted in particular as the potential site of further abuse and violence to both women and children where the risk of serious harm is heightened'.[37] Indeed, James-Hanman and Holt state that, 'child contact arrangements can provide court authorised opportunities for abuse to continue'.[38] Given that there is 'burgeoning empirical evidence which exposes the complex, challenging and potentially dangerous risks of post-separation contact with abusive fathers for both children and their mothers', as Holt remarks, 'it would seem imperative that some degree of caution is applied when decisions are being made about contact for children with domestically abusive men'.[39]

36 For example, Schneider E.M., *Battered Women and Feminist Lawmaking*, 2000, Yale University Press, London, at 52.

37 MacDonald G.S., 'Domestic violence and private family court proceedings: Promoting child welfare or promoting contact?' (2016) 22 *Violence Against Women* 832 at 832.

38 James-Hanman D. and Holt S., 'Post-Separation Contact and Domestic Violence: Our 7-Point Plan for Safe(r) Contact for Children' (2021) 36 *Journal of Family Violence* 991 at 992.

39 Holt S., 'A voice or a choice: Children's views on participating in decisions about post-separation contact with domestically abusive fathers' (2018) 40 *Journal of Social Welfare and Family Law* 459 at 459. For further discussion of child contact in the context of domestic abuse, see also, Burton M., 'Specialist domestic violence courts for child arrangement cases: Safer courtrooms and safer outcomes?' (2018) 40 *Journal of Social Welfare and Family Law* 533; Mackay K., 'The approach in Scotland to child contact disputes involving allegations of domestic abuse' (2018) 40 *Journal of Social Welfare and Family Law* 477; Jeffries S., 'In the best interests of the abuser: Coercive control. Child custody proceedings and the "expert" assessments that guide judicial determinations' (2016) 5 *Laws* 1; Morrison F., 'All over now? The ongoing relational consequences of domestic abuse through children's contact arrangements' (2015) 24 *Child Abuse Review* 274; Barnett A., 'Contact at all costs? Domestic violence and children's welfare' (2014) 26 *Child and Family Law Quarterly* 439; and Holt S., 'A case of laying down the law: Post-separation child contact and domestic abuse' (2011) 4 *Irish Journal of Family Law* 87.

In *I.M. and Others v. Italy*,[40] the applicants, who were a mother and her two children, argued that they had been the victims of domestic abuse and that the state had failed in its duty to protect and assist them during contact sessions with the children's father, who was accused of ill-treatment and threatening behaviour during the sessions. The mother also complained of being deemed an 'uncooperative parent' and of having her parental responsibility suspended, the reason being that she had sought to protect her children by highlighting the risk to their safety. The ECtHR held that there had been a breach of Article 8 in respect of the children, as they had been forced to meet their father in conditions which did not provide a protective environment and therefore their best interests had been disregarded. There had, in addition, been a violation of Article 8 in respect of the children's mother. The domestic courts had failed to examine her situation with care and had decided to suspend her parental responsibility without taking into consideration all of the relevant factors. No account had been taken of the situation of abuse experienced by the first applicant and her children, or of the criminal proceedings which were pending against the children's father for ill-treatment.

The facts of *I.M. and Others v. Italy* could be said to be representative of the type of situation in which issues surrounding child contact in the context of domestic abuse typically arise. Cases involving such issues tend to involve an alleged perpetrator of domestic abuse seeking contact with their children, with the alleged victim and, in some cases, the children being reluctant to engage with contact arrangements due to safety concerns. However, issues surrounding child contact in a domestic abuse context can also arise in other types of situations. In contrast to *I.M. and Others v. Italy*, the case of *Luca v. Moldova*[41] related to an alleged failure of the state authorities to protect the applicant from domestic abuse and to support her in maintaining contact with her children. According to the applicant, her husband (referred to in the judgment as A.I.) had, from around 2015, subjected her to incidents of physical and psychological abuse. In August 2016, a protection order was issued, stating that A.I. had to refrain from contact with the applicant and their two children. The applicant alleged to the police that A.I. had broken the terms of this order; however, no investigation was opened. When the applicant sought an extension of the protection order, the national courts rejected the application. In July 2016, the applicant made a criminal complaint against A.I., alleging physical abuse. A.I. was given an administrative fine by the police, but no

40 (App. No. 25426/20), judgment of 10 November 2022.

41 (App. No. 55351/17), judgment of 17 October 2023. For discussion of this case, see McQuigg R., 'Child Contact and Domestic Abuse' (2024) *European Human Rights Law Review* 177; and McQuigg R., 'Domestic Abuse and Child Contact: *Luca v. The Republic of Moldova*', 14 November 2023, https://strasbourgobservers.com/2023/11/14/domestic-abuse-and-child-contact-luca-v-the-republic-of-moldova/.

investigation was opened at that time. Investigations into two other allegations against A.I. by the applicant, including domestic abuse, were opened at a later stage, resulting in A.I. being convicted, given a suspended prison sentence and ordered to pay damages. In August 2016, the children moved in with A.I. and contact between the applicant and the children ceased. The applicant sought assistance, but the child protection authority refused to issue a contact schedule. The applicant went to the courts and obtained a contact-schedule order, but A.I. allegedly refused to abide by it. The applicant and A.I. divorced in March 2022. The applicant alleged that the authorities had failed to protect her from domestic abuse and to assist her in maintaining her relationship with her children when they had left to live with their father. The applicant also argued that the authorities' inaction had been a result of her being a woman and of complacency in relation to domestic abuse.

In relation to the applicant's complaint that the authorities had failed to protect her from domestic abuse, the ECtHR found that the authorities had failed in their obligation 'to carry out an immediate and proactive assessment of the risk of recurrent violence against the applicant and to take operational and preventive measures to mitigate that risk, to protect the applicant and to condemn the perpetrator's conduct'.[42] There had thus been a breach of Article 3. As regards the applicant's allegation that the authorities had failed to assist her in maintaining contact with her children, she submitted that the children had been taken away by their father and had subsequently been manipulated by him, resulting in their refusal to have any contact with her. The applicant argued that the child protection authority had not provided any support in time to prevent the children's further estrangement and had not assessed the reasons for their hostility despite the context of domestic abuse. The ECtHR found that the authorities had afforded no consideration to the applicant's accounts of having had normal relations with her children before they had moved in with their father or to the domestic abuse. The Court accepted that 'on a practical basis, there may indeed come a stage where it becomes futile, if not counterproductive and harmful, to attempt to force a child to conform to a situation which, for whatever reasons, he or she resists'.[43] However, although 'coercive measures against children are not desirable and must be limited in this sensitive area',[44] nevertheless the applicant 'was left to defend her right to maintain contact with her children by her own efforts, including by initiating court proceedings against the authorities that were meant to provide her with support'.[45] There was no indication that 'the authorities had any awareness of or sensitivity to the applicant's vulnerability as a victim of domestic

42 At para. 74.
43 At para. 94.
44 At para. 94.
45 At para. 94.

violence'.[46] Given the failure of the authorities to take into account the context of domestic abuse in the determination of child contact rights and to take prompt measures to support the applicant in maintaining contact with her children, the ECtHR found that there had been a breach of Article 8.

Interestingly, on the same date that the ECtHR issued its judgment in *Luca*, the Court issued a further judgment against the same state in another case involving child contact and domestic abuse. In *Bîzdîga v. Moldova*,[47] a protection order had been issued against the applicant in March 2016 due to a number of incidents of psychological abuse against his then-wife (who was referred to in the judgment as C). The couple divorced in June 2016, and C was awarded custody of their child. The applicant sought a contact arrangement, and the child protection authority approved a schedule of two hours' contact per week at the child's home. On appeal, contact was extended to four hours per week. In November 2016, the applicant brought court proceedings seeking more contact hours, but without success. After several incidents in which he was unable to see his child, the applicant complained to the child protection authority. In December 2017, the applicant sought a change of custody but was unsuccessful. The ECtHR stated that it was 'not satisfied that the decision-making process, as a result of which the applicant's contact rights were limited, was reasonable, fair and sufficiently expedient in the circumstances of the case'.[48] In particular, 'the alleged history of domestic violence was a relevant and mandatory factor to be weighed in the assessment of domestic authorities when deciding on contact rights'.[49] However, sufficient consideration did not seem to have been afforded to this factor, and thus the applicant had not been given a fair chance to make his case. There had therefore been a breach of Article 8. The ECtHR also held that there had been a violation of Article 6 of the ECHR,[50] as the domestic courts had not genuinely examined the admissibility of the application before them and had not given reasons for its rejection. The applicant had thus suffered a disproportionate restriction on his right of access to a court in breach of Article 6(1).

The facts of *Bîzdîga* are somewhat different from those of *Luca*, in that the applicant in *Bîzdîga* had been the subject of allegations of domestic abuse as opposed to being the alleged victim of such abuse. Nevertheless, the judgments in both cases, along with that in *I.M. and Others v. Italy*, demonstrate a meritorious recognition on the part of the ECtHR of the importance of

46 At para. 94.
47 (App. No. 15646/18), judgment of 17 October 2023.
48 At para. 69.
49 At para. 62.
50 Article 6(1) provides that, 'In the determination of his civil rights and obligations or of any criminal charge against him, everyone is entitled to a fair and public hearing within a reasonable time by an independent and impartial tribunal established by law'.

affording sufficient consideration to allegations of domestic abuse in any case involving child contact.

Conclusion

In conclusion, therefore, it is certainly the case that Article 8 tended to be used more extensively in the earlier jurisprudence of the ECtHR on domestic abuse. If addressing the responses of criminal justice systems to domestic abuse, the Court is now much more likely to base its findings on Article 3 or, in situations in which such abuse has resulted in a fatality, on Article 2, as well as frequently finding a violation of Article 14. However, in recent times, the Court has found breaches of Article 8 in cases involving the use of cyberviolence in situations of domestic abuse, as has been discussed. Also, whilst the Court's early case law on domestic abuse focused almost exclusively on the responses of criminal justice systems, this body of jurisprudence has now evolved to encompass other aspects of state responses to such abuse. Indeed, the fact that the ECtHR's jurisprudence on domestic abuse has now reached a stage whereby it encompasses detailed consideration of a specific issue, such as child contact in this context, demonstrates the extent to which the Court's understanding of the issue of domestic abuse has now developed.

6 Conclusions

This book has sought to provide a detailed exploration of the jurisprudence of the ECtHR on domestic abuse. Although traditionally this was not an issue that was regarded as falling within the ambit of international human rights law, as was discussed in Chapter 1, through the development of the concepts of state responsibility and positive obligations, human rights law has now evolved to encompass domestic abuse. For example, in its General Recommendations Nos. 19[1] and 35,[2] the CEDAW Committee interpreted CEDAW, which contains no express reference to violence against women, in such a manner as to encompass such violence in both the public and private spheres. Within regional systems of human rights protection, the Convention of Belém do Pará was adopted by the General Assembly of the Organization of American States in 1994; the Maputo Protocol, which encompasses *inter alia* violence against women, was adopted by the African Union in 2003; and in 2011 the Council of Europe adopted the Istanbul Convention.

However, the focus of this book was on developments in the jurisprudence of the ECtHR on domestic abuse. Through the application of the concept of positive obligations, it has now been established that such abuse can constitute a violation of the right to life under Article 2 of the ECHR, the right to be free from torture or inhuman or degrading treatment under Article 3, the right to respect for private and family life under Article 8 and the prohibition of discrimination found in Article 14.

An important theme of this book was how conceptualisations of domestic abuse in the jurisprudence of the ECtHR have evolved. As was discussed in Chapter 2, in the Court's early case law on domestic abuse, its approach to the use of Articles 3 and 8 was somewhat incoherent, in terms of on which provision it based its findings of violations of the ECHR. Essentially the ECtHR seemed to take the view that if a breach was found, it did not matter to any

1 UN Committee on the Elimination of Discrimination Against Women, 'General Recommendation No. 19: Violence against women' (1992).
2 UN Committee on the Elimination of Discrimination Against Women, 'General Recommendation No. 35: Gender-based violence against women' (2017).

DOI: 10.4324/9781003493068-6

great extent whether the abuse in question was conceptualised as a violation of Article 3 or as a breach of Article 8. It is likely that the Court's apparent preference for the use of Article 8 as opposed to Article 3 in its early jurisprudence on this issue was due simply to the fact that it can be more straightforward to establish a violation of Article 8 than it is to establish a breach of Article 3. However, in *Valiuliene v. Lithuania*,[3] the state argued that the ill-treatment to which the applicant, a victim of domestic abuse, had been subjected had not been sufficiently severe to fall within the ambit of Article 3, and presented the ECtHR with a unilateral declaration acknowledging a breach of Article 8. The Court refused to accept this declaration, found a violation of Article 3 and stated that it was not necessary to examine the complaint under Article 8, as a breach of Article 3 had already been found. It seems that the case of *Valiuliene* served to highlight to the ECtHR that an important issue in domestic abuse cases is not only whether a violation of the ECHR is found, but also on which provision such a finding is based. Indeed, this case marked a change in the Court's approach and henceforth Article 3 was used much more extensively in such cases.

However, it is argued that although conceptualisations of domestic abuse in the case law of the ECtHR have evolved greatly in a very meritorious manner, further development of the Court's conceptualisation of this issue is still needed. Despite the fact that it has now been firmly established that domestic abuse falls within the scope of Article 3, the Court has not yet found expressly in any case involving domestic abuse that such abuse violates the 'torture' limb of this provision, as distinguished from 'inhuman or degrading treatment'. In *Volodina v. Russia*[4] and *Tunikova and Others v. Russia*,[5] both of which involved domestic abuse, questions arose as to whether the ECtHR should have expressly found violations of the 'torture' limb of Article 3, and Chapter 2 included discussion of the potential merits of such a finding in a domestic abuse case.

The way in which Article 3 is used in the jurisprudence of the ECtHR on domestic abuse has certainly evolved greatly, from an approach whereby the Court tended instead to apply Article 8 in such cases to a situation whereby the use of Article 3 is commonplace. Also, the Court has now shown a clear awareness that domestic abuse is not only constituted by physical violence, and that wider patterns of coercive control such as psychological abuse can also come within the ambit of Article 3.[6] Indeed the debate has now become whether domestic abuse should be expressly conceptualised by the ECtHR as

3 (App. No. 33234/07), judgment of 26 March 2013.
4 (App. No. 41261/17), judgment of 9 July 2019.
5 (App. Nos. 55974/16, 53118/17, 27484/18, 28011/19), judgment of 14 December 2021.
6 See, for example, *Volodina v. Russia* (App. No. 41261/17), judgment of 9 July 2019, at para. 75.

torture. It seems that such a finding would be meritorious in terms of making a strong statement regarding the seriousness of such abuse.

Chapter 3 developed the theme of the ECtHR's evolving conceptualisation of domestic abuse by focusing on a further facet of this – namely the Court's approach to domestic abuse as a form of gender-based discrimination under Article 14. The use of this provision in such cases has expanded greatly in recent years, which is reflective of the increased use of Article 14 by the ECtHR generally. The Court has very clearly conceptualised domestic abuse as a form of gender-based discrimination, and in doing so has followed the approach of the UN bodies such as the CEDAW Committee in this respect. Essentially, once an applicant has brought forth evidence such as statistics to demonstrate that domestic abuse affects women disproportionately in the respondent state, it then falls upon the authorities to show that they deployed effective remedial measures to address that disadvantage. Should the state fail to demonstrate that such action has been taken, a breach of Article 14 will be found by the ECtHR.

A prominent theme in this book was the evolution of the ECtHR's understanding of domestic abuse. As was discussed in Chapter 4, in its judgment in *Kurt v. Austria*,[7] the Grand Chamber set out a number of key principles that should be applied by the ECtHR when considering cases involving domestic abuse, particularly in the context of Article 2. In this judgment, the Grand Chamber addressed the important question that had arisen in previous cases regarding how the *Osman* test should be applied in the context of domestic abuse.[8] In *Osman*, it was established that in appropriate circumstances, Article 2 places a positive duty on the state to take preventive operational measures to protect an individual whose life is at risk from the criminal acts of another individual. However, for such a positive duty to arise, it must be established that the relevant authorities knew or ought to have known at the time of the existence of 'a real and immediate risk to the life of an identified individual'.[9]

Prior to the Grand Chamber's judgment in *Kurt v. Austria*, a recognition had begun to grow that the application of the *Osman* test in circumstances involving domestic abuse could be problematic, in terms of the need for the authorities to be aware of an 'immediate' risk to life in order for a positive duty to take preventive operational measures to arise.[10] In the context of

7 (App. No. 62903/15), judgment of 15 June 2021.

8 This test is derived from the judgment of the ECtHR in *Osman v. United Kingdom* (App. No. 23452/94), judgment of 28 October 1998.

9 At para. 116.

10 See, for example, *Valiuliene v. Lithuania* (App. No. 33234/07), judgment of 26 March 2013, Concurring Opinion of Judge Pinto de Albuquerque, at para. 31; *Volodina v. Russia* (App. No. 41261/17), judgment of 9 July 2019, Separate Opinion of Judge Pinto de Albuquerque, joined by Judge Dedov, at para. 12; and *Kurt v. Austria* (App. No. 62903/15), judgment of 4 July 2019 (first instance judgment), Concurring Opinion of Judge Huseynov, at paras. 3–4.

domestic abuse, even if a risk to life does not appear to be immediate as such, there is a substantial possibility that this could escalate at any point. In *Kurt v. Austria*, the Grand Chamber established that the 'immediacy' element of the *Osman* test should be interpreted in such a manner as to take account of the specific nature of domestic abuse. The Court's understanding of the dynamics of domestic abuse has certainly developed, as epitomised by the recognition by the Grand Chamber that the *Osman* test must be applied in cases involving domestic abuse in such a way as to take account of the particular context of such abuse.

However, as was discussed in Chapter 4, it is arguable that the way in which the majority of the Grand Chamber proceeded to apply the very meritorious principles articulated in the first part of its judgment to the specific facts of the case in question is problematic. Having established that account must be taken of the particular circumstances of domestic abuse, it seems that the majority may then have failed to take these circumstances into consideration in a sufficient manner. It appears that the dissenting judges may have had a better understanding of the dynamics of domestic abuse than their colleagues in the majority.

Nevertheless, the Grand Chamber's judgment certainly constitutes a landmark in the jurisprudence of the ECtHR on domestic abuse, particularly regarding the Court's use of Article 2 in such cases. Interestingly, the judgment may not result in changes to the ultimate outcomes in many cases. Nevertheless, it appears from the judgments that have since been issued by the ECtHR that henceforth the principles set out by the Grand Chamber will generally be followed closely by the Court in domestic abuse cases involving Article 2, potentially leading to a more uniform approach by the ECtHR in its consideration of such cases. Additionally, the application of these principles could lead to the Court finding breaches in circumstances in which it would not have done so prior to the Grand Chamber's judgment, as may have been the case in *Y and Others v. Bulgaria*.[11]

Chapter 5 examined a number of issues that have arisen in the ECtHR's very recent jurisprudence on domestic abuse, which have been addressed by the Court using Article 8. As noted above, this provision tended to be used more extensively in the earlier jurisprudence of the ECtHR on domestic abuse. When addressing the responses of criminal justice systems to such abuse, the Court is now much more likely to base its findings on Article 3 or, in situations in which such abuse has resulted in a fatality, on Article 2, as well as frequently also finding a violation of Article 14. However, the ECtHR has found violations of Article 8 in the recent cases of *Buturugă v. Romania*[12] and

11 (App. No. 9077/18), judgment of 22 March 2022.

12 (App. No. 56867/15), judgment of 11 February 2020. A violation of Article 3 was also found in this case.

Volodina v. Russia (No. 2),[13] both of which involved the very current issue of cyberviolence. In recent times, there has been a growing recognition of the ways in which perpetrators may use technology in their abuse, and Chapter 5 analysed the Court's approach to this issue.

Also, whilst the Court's early case law on domestic abuse focused almost exclusively on the responses of criminal justice systems, this body of jurisprudence has now evolved to encompass other aspects of state responses to such abuse, as seen in *J.D. and A v. United Kingdom*,[14] which was discussed in Chapter 3 and *Levchuk v. Ukraine*,[15] which was analysed in Chapter 5. These cases related to the housing situations of victims of domestic abuse and are of particular importance given that it has been argued that the most important needs of victims of domestic abuse are for social support measures, such as monetary resources, refuge accommodation and housing.[16] As was discussed in Chapter 3, the rights contained in the ECHR largely fall within the category of 'civil and political' rights, as opposed to 'socioeconomic' rights, and there are generally limits on what courts can achieve. For example, as Chayes remarks, it is substantially more difficult for courts to order that affirmative programmes be put in place than it is for them to hold that certain practices be halted.[17] Nevertheless, the judgment in *J.D. and A* related to ensuring that a victim of domestic abuse could remain in her home in which a 'panic room' had been installed, whilst the decision in *Levchuk* related to ensuring the eviction of a perpetrator of domestic abuse from the home of the victim. Both cases therefore related to ensuring the safety of victims in terms of their living arrangements. Although it is unlikely that the ECtHR would hold specifically that refuges should be built, it would seem that it would not constitute a great leap from its judgments in *J.D. and A* and *Levchuk* for the Court to order that steps should be taken to rehouse victims of abuse.

As was also discussed in Chapter 5, violations of Article 8 were found in *I.M. and Others v. Italy*[18] and *Luca v. Moldova*,[19] both of which related to issues surrounding child contact in the context of domestic abuse. Again, given that the early case law of the ECtHR on domestic abuse focused almost exclusively on the responses of police and prosecutors, the fact that this body of jurisprudence has now reached a stage whereby it encompasses detailed consideration of a specific issue, such as child contact in this context,

13 (App. No. 40419/19), judgment of 14 September 2021.
14 (App. Nos. 32949/17, 34614/17), judgment of 24 October 2019.
15 (App. No. 17496/19), judgment of 3 September 2020.
16 For example, Schneider E.M., *Battered Women and Feminist Lawmaking*, 2000, Yale University Press, London, at 52.
17 Chayes A., 'The Role of the Judge in Public Law Litigation', (1976) 89 *Harvard Law Review* 1281 at 1295–1296.
18 (App. No. 25426/20), judgment of 10 November 2022.
19 (App. No. 55351/17), judgment of 17 October 2023.

demonstrates the extent to which the Court's understanding of domestic abuse has now evolved.

It is certainly true to say that a considerable body of important jurisprudence on domestic abuse has been developed by the ECtHR. Given that it was not until 2007 that such abuse was given substantive consideration by the Court,[20] this body of case law has therefore been amassed within a relatively short space of time. The ways in which the ECtHR has conceptualised domestic abuse have evolved and are likely to develop further in the future. In particular, such abuse may be expressly conceptualised by the ECtHR as torture, a development that would serve to emphasise the seriousness of this issue. Likewise, it is argued that the Court's understanding of the dynamics of domestic abuse has evolved, as epitomised by the recognition by the Grand Chamber in *Kurt v. Austria* that the *Osman* test must be applied in cases involving domestic abuse in such a manner as to take account of the particular context of such abuse. The ECtHR has also demonstrated a willingness to develop its jurisprudence on domestic abuse beyond exclusively addressing issues relating to criminal justice responses, and it is argued that the Court should continue and expand this approach, particularly as the primary needs of victims may be for social support measures. Overall, the ECtHR is to be commended for its willingness to develop its approaches to domestic abuse. It remains to be seen how the Court's jurisprudence on this important issue will evolve further in the future.

20 *Kontrova v. Slovakia* (App. No. 7510/04), judgment of 31 May 2007.

Index

For Product Safety Concerns and Information please contact our EU
representative GPSR@taylorandfrancis.com Taylor & Francis Verlag GmbH,
Kaufingerstraße 24, 80331 München, Germany

Printed and bound by CPI Group (UK) Ltd, Croydon, CR0 4YY
14/09/2026
02216256-0003